THE PERFECT CLOSET

AND OTHER STORAGE IDEAS

Debra K. Melchior

Publications International, Ltd.

Debra K. Melchior originated and operated The Debbinaire Way, a space organization and consulting company. Ms. Melchior is the author of *Organize Your Home* and has spoken on television and radio and to community groups on making the most of available living and storage spaces.

Photo credits:
Front cover: **The Closet® Factory** (bottom); **Department of Public Affairs Lillian Vernon Corporation** (left); **Sam Griffith Studio** (right).
Back cover: **Sam Griffith Studio. The Closet® Factory:** 35, 77, 83, 95, 123, 127; **K. Christian/Photogroup/FPG International:** 128; **Closet™ Works:** 5, 8, 10, 55, 56 (left), 57, 61, 78, 91, 120; **Department of**

Public Affairs Lillian Vernon Corporation: 22, 26, 28, 33, 41, 46, 47, 49, 56 (bottom), 58, 99, 112; **Metro:** 37; **Sam Griffith Studio:** 7 (top), 9, 13, 16, 19, 89, 105, 109, 110, 115, 116, 118, 119, 126; **Spacial Designs: Jay Daniels:** 7 (bottom); **Thomas Jacobs:** 38.

Illustrations: Mark Pechenik: 15, 80, 86, 90, 96, 100.

The brand name products mentioned or shown in this publication are service marks or trademarks of their respective companies. Mention of these products in text, photographs, or directions is for demonstration purposes only and does not constitute an endorsement of Publications International, Ltd.

TABLE OF
CONTENTS

TAKE CHARGE
OF YOUR
CLOSET

Many years ago, people kept their belongings on a few pegs or nails scattered around their living quarters. The overflow was stored in trunks and chests. Apparently, this arrangement was not completely satisfactory, because the passage of time brought cupboards, armoires, cabinets, buffets, and wardrobes. Eventually, someone thought of setting aside separate rooms or nooks for storing possessions. This area was called a closet: whether a butler's closet, coat closet, linen closet, or clothing closet. As time moved on, the accumulation of material goods became greater, and the cost of individual items increased dramatically. People were forced to pay greater attention to protecting and caring for their possessions.

A few years ago, the concept of "space management" and the appearance of "organizing consultants" appeared on the scene, causing people to reevaluate their belongings and their storage space. Now, the idea of changing and improving storage space through remodeling has caught on everywhere. Today, marketing techniques and media exposure influence people's thoughts on the subject of storage. As each new and innovative storage product comes to market, awareness and desire grow for beautiful, spacious closets and

A closet in disarray makes a chore out of an easy task such as finding a matching pair of shoes.

storage areas. People explore each magnificent home in newer developments, hoping to examine the newest developments in "space efficiency."

When people return to their own homes, they become disappointed and displeased with the clutter and confusion they find there. But that  doesn't mean selling your house and moving to a bigger one. It does mean evaluating your present storage situation and seeking a solution. The clutter in your house is not the result of any flaw or omission on your part. The concept of space conservation is relatively new, but now you can do something about the clutter in your house. *The Perfect Closet and Other Storage Ideas* will help you reach your goal of a neat and more spacious home. The disorganization of your closets isn't going to go away, and it will annoy you until you do something about it. So read on and get organized!

From nails and pegs on walls, organizing has advanced to elaborate walk-in closets (above) and workshop spaces (left). Space management and organization can be applied to any situation by anyone.

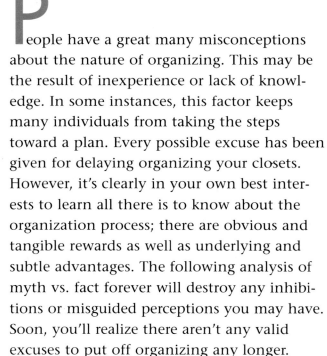

CHAPTER 1

GETTING
STARTED

Stacked shelves help shoe storage become second nature.

People have a great many misconceptions about the nature of organizing. This may be the result of inexperience or lack of knowledge. In some instances, this factor keeps many individuals from taking the steps toward a plan. Every possible excuse has been given for delaying organizing your closets. However, it's clearly in your own best interests to learn all there is to know about the organization process; there are obvious and tangible rewards as well as underlying and subtle advantages. The following analysis of myth vs. fact forever will destroy any inhibitions or misguided perceptions you may have. Soon, you'll realize there aren't any valid excuses to put off organizing any longer.

When clothes are arranged evenly along a rod, wrinkles are eliminated and clothes are more visible.

ORGANIZING: MYTH AND FACT

MYTH: "I need more rooms, more closets, and more storage space before I can get organized."

FACT: By organizing the space you have, you gain the extra room, closet, or storage area you're seeking.

ANALYSIS: If you don't learn how to store your belongings and possessions wisely and conscientiously, you'll soon outgrow a house even the size of Buckingham Palace. It isn't the amount of space you have, but how you use it that counts. Although some homes can't supply even a meager place to begin the organization process, you can still create your own storage area from scratch.

This transparent door shelving unit is just one of the many items that make organizing your closet much easier today.

MYTH: "I just did my spring cleaning, so I'm in good shape for another year or until it's so messy again I can't stand it."

FACT: Organizing is not synonymous with spring cleaning or with periodic attempts to straighten up.

ANALYSIS: Proper organizing is a one-time project. With careful planning, you'll never restack, refold, or rearrange again. Good organizing creates a maintenance-free system that uses your daily routines to keep it in the same pristine condition as the day you finished organizing it. A beneficial by-product of organizing is that it counteracts and controls the bad habits that contributed to the clutter you now face.

MYTH: "I just paid a small fortune to have my closet 'organized,' so why is it a mess again?"

FACT: The closet wasn't "organized," it was remodeled. New shelves and closet rods can fall victim to the same disorder and disarray as readily as did the old ones.

ANALYSIS: Perhaps once the installation was complete, no one explained how to place your garments and accessories in the newly remodeled closet. If you did the remodeling yourself, new hardware won't change the difficulties you've been facing with clutter. Learning the principles of organizing will lay the groundwork for using your newly organized closet to meet your needs.

MYTH: "I must have too many clothes and not enough closet space because I waste time every day trying to find what I'm looking for. I spend far too much money on my wardrobe and my dry cleaning bill is exorbitant, but every day I have to iron my outfit because it's so wrinkled when I take it out of the closet. I just don't have the time to do anything about this problem."

FACT: Organizing arranges your clothing evenly along the clothes rod, eliminating the crowded, crammed conditions that cause your clothing to wrinkle. Organizing positions clothing and accessories for instant visibility and accessibility.

ANALYSIS: Once you can see the clothes you own, future purchases will probably be more effective. You're more likely to buy a piece that blends with your existing wardrobe rather than buying a whole new outfit. That bargain buy won't seem like a bargain when you realize you already own three similar articles. Organizing shows the same old clothes in a new light, increasing versatility and wearability. It also saves time. There will be no more needless trips to the cleaners and the ironing board, no more standing in front of the closet trying to remember what was supposed to go to the cleaners, and no more relentless searching of the closet and the dresser drawer for the desired item.

MYTH: "It's easier to buy another one of what I need than to spend half the day searching for the one that is out in the garage somewhere."

FACT: Repeatedly purchasing the same items and products is a common occurrence when you're disorganized. It is an admission of defeat, since you've allowed the clutter to control you rather than you taking control of the clutter. Repeated purchases also perpetuate the original problem of too much clutter.

ANALYSIS: Organizing systematically and methodically assigns a specific place for everything. You then know exactly and precisely where everything is. It will be easy to find a given item, and you'll put it away in the same place.

MYTH: "I really do want to get organized, but it's just too much of a disaster after 15 years in the same house."

FACT: You've allowed yourself to be intimidated by the very prospect of organizing. Years of procrastination haven't helped; instead, try to break this pattern. Take a little more time and read every page of this book.

ANALYSIS: You're understandably overwhelmed, but that's because you've been viewing the chaotic conditions in their entirety. Break down the whole into smaller and more manageable parts. Then evaluate each smaller area of clutter and determine how to conquer it effectively. Gradually, every section of the house—taking one closet, one cabinet, one corner at a time—will come under control.

MYTH: "I don't know what to keep and what to throw away."

FACT: No one can give you a definitive answer. Some books on the subject of "clutter" try to coerce you to follow their set of standards. But *The Perfect Closet and Other Storage Ideas* deals with handling all your belongings, not just what's left after shoveling most of it out of the way.

Routine use should reinforce the organizing system: Here, ties are hung in the same area as dress shirts.

ANALYSIS: For whatever reason, people seem compelled to stockpile their possessions. That's OK as long as they devise a system to accommodate them; you don't want the "stockpile" to get in the way of two or three frequently used items. If you find yourself continually rummaging through an "organized" area, your system isn't working and you need to try again.

YOU NEED A PLAN

The hardest step to take is *committing* yourself to the first organizing project. After that, the rest is easy; it's simply a matter of learning the principles of organizing, following a sensible sequence in organizing, and visualizing and defining a precise objective.

You have two options for organizing: You can either do it yourself or call in a professional organizer. Most professional organizing companies are limited to dealing with closets or garages, leaving the rest of the house to your own devices. Some companies may help with custom cabinetry for dens, kitchens, or bathrooms, and their professional designers can help with pricing and selection of materials. But this type of help has little or nothing to do with the principles of organizing.

Evaluate each of the areas you plan to organize and determine which one causes the most distress. Begin by organizing that area. If you are using outside help, formulate a list of specific requirements you consider vital to the good use of the space, the protection of your possessions, and your own peace of mind. It's a good idea to consult with two or three different organizing firms before choosing one. And do some research on your own to gain as much knowledge of the subject as possible. Don't be hesitant about discussing and listening to suggestions; the more information and strategies you digest, the better the outcome will be.

Remember, you have the final word on every decision. Don't automatically accede to every recommendation the representative makes unless you understand and agree with

A visual closet design is necessary to evaluate whether your idea will accommodate your storage needs.

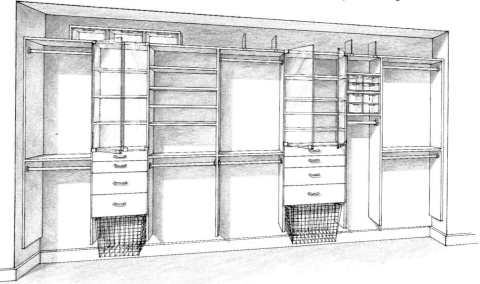

Keeping shorter jackets and coats on separate rods from longer outerwear will save you the frustration of separating an unorganized mound at the end of the season.

the reason for its inclusion. (Do the same for your own personal design.) You will regret it later if you simply turn the matter over to a consultant. You must be involved, since only you know your needs and preferences.

The underlying key to success is having a clear, well-conceived plan, whether the plan is your own or a scheme designed by you and the organizer/designer. If you act hastily, you may have a tendency to disregard the planning stage. If you don't have a plan, you'll probably end up taking everything out of the closet. This will leave you frustrated, discontent, and with a formidable mound of stuff piled on the floor.

With a carefully crafted plan, you can look forward to a smooth and swift process. Remember this simple equation: The more time spent planning, the less time and money spent later in physical labor and correcting mistakes.

Investigate the impact of the following elements of organizing. These elements bring sparkle, refinement, practicality, and common sense to the area being organized.

Simplicity. Conserving space is important, but not if it makes the system harder to operate than a system using a little more space. Keep it simple; a system that isn't being used isn't a system at all, no matter how much space is conserved.

Consistency. The ultimate goal is to use methods that can be maintained without any extra effort on your part. The system should be designed in such a way that your daily, routine use of the system keeps it in order.

Compromise. Few things in life, including organizing a closet, can be attained without some amount of compromise. You may have to forfeit advantages in one area to achieve advantages in another.

Propaganda. "Let the buyer beware" is an apt warning for consumers to heed. Manufacturers display a constant stream of new products and gadgets for "organizing." Don't be swayed or confused by advertising or the myriad products on the market. Decide what you need and then search the marketplace for the product or materials that will do the job.

CHAPTER 2

WORKING WITHIN YOUR
LIMITS

B efore exploring and learning the finer points of the organizing process, as well as the detailed and specific information required to carry any project to a successful conclusion, a few general guidelines must be followed. These guidelines will highlight some of the underlying reasons for past disappointments with your closets. The guidelines will also show how people unknowingly contribute to creating a problematic closet. Until these hidden factors are recognized and new perceptions of organizing embraced, any attempt at closet organizing will fall short of your goals.

A spacious, accommodating closet isn't obtained by merely increasing its size or installing

High heels use more vertical space than flat-heeled shoes. Keep such limitations in mind when organizing.

new shelves and rods. The biggest closet imaginable, with beautiful closet appointments, would soon become an unruly jumble unless the principles of organizing are understood. Rather than let your closet control you, these organizing principles will allow you to control your closet.

The first principle of organizing is to assign your clothes and accessories to specific locations inside your closet. Observing these original assignments virtually guarantees that this regulated placement will continue. The trick comes in determining how and where to place your belongings in the closet. Since different clothes and accessories possess completely different characteristics, you cannot treat them as one entity. Also, individuals have personal preferences for storing clothes, and people come in different proportions, sizes, and shapes. And closets range in size from minuscule to mammoth. These factors drastically affect the closet's layout, the materials installed, and the storage systems selected.

Many garments must be hung from the rods of your closet. Others are perfectly suited to alternative methods of storage. It is important to properly identify and classify your garments to provide them with sufficient space, whether it is rod space, shelf space, floor space, or on a specialty rack.

Slacks provide a good example of personal preference in storage. When slacks are hung lengthwise from the cuff rather than folded over a hanger, the vertical length occupied by the slacks precludes the possibility of double-rodding. This squanders a vast amount of otherwise usable space.

Shoes exemplify how a person's size and shape affect closet design. A pair of men's shoes may demand more storage space than a pair of women's shoes. Don't assume each and every shoe rack on the market will serve both sizes. They don't. Be sure to examine any potential purchase of closet materials to make certain it can accommodate your size.

A closet with a sloped or lower-than-normal ceiling, masonry/plaster/brick walls rather than wall board, windows, or vents or other unusual structural components will restrict the materials that you may be able to use. The shape and size of your closet may also limit the location and installation of any organizing materials you buy. Use careful consideration. Before making any purchases, draw an exact replica of your closet, including its positive and negative features.

UNEXPLORED RESOURCES IN YOUR CLOSET

The type or style of your closet door is a factor (seldom thought of) that can tremendously increase the capacity of your closet. The position of the door can be either a hindrance or a help because it determines whether the adjoining wall space (on the inside of your closet) is accessible or large enough to be used in some way. The wall space on either side of the door and above the door can often supply an abundant area of usable space; yet more often than not, it is overlooked. Depending on the amount and accessibility of the available space, many things can be done to

A closet has its storage limits, but also contains much unused space. Everyday drip-dry clips can hold items such as boots or bags on wall hooks.

The closet door itself has many storage possibilities. This shoe bag will hold up to 12 pairs of shoes. Some shoe bags will fit 18 or 21 pairs.

convert it into a self-contained storage system.

One possible use for this extra wall space is for storing boots. Install hooks of one variety or another in a configuration that matches the length and width of your various pairs of boots. Each pair of boots can then be hung from a standard drip-dry clip that hangs from an installed hook. The boots are no longer underfoot on the closet floor or occupying valuable shelf space that could be used for other purposes.

A second option is to use "cubbyholes" in all or part of this newly discovered area. Cubbyholes work wonderfully for keeping stacks of sweaters conveniently contained and categorized or for keeping pocketbooks, handbags, and purses in an upright position for easy access. This method allows you to clearly see each pocketbook, handbag, and purse without digging through various layers. Again, this option opens up shelf space inside the closet, since a large volume of handbags and/or sweaters and knits have been removed, and now a larger area of the closet is available for another use.

The closet door itself—if it is a standard open-in/open-out door rather than a pocket door, sliding doors, bi-fold doors, or no door at all—can also be useful for storage. But don't discount those other door styles entirely; they may supply enough storage to warrant an investigation into their potential.

Typically, the inside of the closet door works well for belt racks, scarves, necklaces, and other articles meant to be hung. Laundry bags are not appropriate here. Any type of storage rack that is bulky or protrudes is going to get in the way, or it could brush against the clothes inside the closet when the door is closed.

A handy convenience for the inside of a closet door is the over-the-door shoe bag or rack, especially one that holds 18 or 21 pairs of shoes. Those shoes in their boxes on the shelf occupy anywhere from 42 inches to 147 inches of horizontal shelf space, depending on whether the boxes are stacked or sitting side by side. When you convert your closet door into a shoe display, more shelf space becomes available while the shoes become more visible and accessible.

CLOTHES CONSCIOUS

You will need to take an accurate and detailed inventory of all articles that belong in your closet. Without an inventory, you will be unable to designate priorities and incapable of determining the amount of space you should allot for each category. When the inventory is almost complete, you will have gained invaluable information about your belongings. As you finish your inventory, there will be no room for error in your design because the numbers will be right in front of you. To complete your inventory, three issues need to be resolved.

First, are there seasonal clothes stored in other closets, trunks, or elsewhere that might serve you better if they were incorporated into your main clothes closet? An organized closet increases your closet's capacity to hold additional pieces of your wardrobe. Decide which of your seasonal garments can actually be worn more months out of the year.

Second, your main closet usually contains many items that don't belong there. Remove every item from your closet that has nothing to do with your daily life or that isn't worn frequently. This includes clothing you thought might fit you in the future, items you intend to donate to charity, and clothes you think might come back in style again. Sort through the discarded merchandise and separate it into distinct categories, assigning each category to a location elsewhere in your home. These discarded articles could include pieces of your wardrobe that are more exotic, such as ball gowns, boas, beaded bags, and tuxedos. If these items are seldom worn, they should be con-

Your chart should include all categories of clothes and a separate column for lengths when appropriate.

INVENTORY CHART

	FEMALE		MALE	
Belts	____		____	
Blazers/Jackets	____	____ in.	____	____ in.
Blouses/Shirts	____	____ in.	____	____ in.
Boots (Tall)	____	____ in.	____	____ in.
Boots (Short)	____	____ in.	____	____ in.
Dresses (Street)	____	____ in.	____	
Dresses (Formal)	____	____ in.	____	
Hats/Visors	____		____	
Jogging Sweats	____		____	
Jumpsuits	____	____ in.	____	
Purses	____		____	
Robes (Nightwear)	____	____ in.	____	____ in.
Shoes	____		____	
Skirts	____		____	
Slacks	____		____	____ in.
Suits	____		____	____ in.
Ties/Scarves	____		____	
Super Bulky Sweaters	____		____	
Reg. Bulky Sweaters	____		____	
T-Shirts	____		____	

signed to a closet other than your everyday clothes closet.

Third, measure the lengths of your garments from the top of the closet rod to the bottom edge of the garment itself. This important piece of information tells you how much vertical space is required for slacks, dresses, or suits, so they can hang without obstruction. Remember, individuals come in all shapes and sizes. This affects the lengths of the clothing you possess. Clothing style and personal taste also affect garment length. For instance, whether your skirts and dresses are mini or calf length makes a big difference. A final factor to consider when measuring

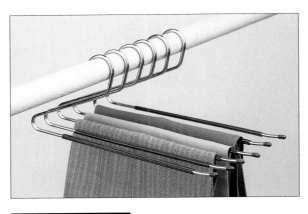

Chrome hangers save space by placing your garments closer to the clothing rod.

garment length is the type of hanger your clothes hang from; this can dramatically alter your closet design. Chrome hangers position a garment three to four inches closer to the rod than a conventional hanger, giving your closet more vertical space.

Following is a list of average lengths for various garments. This should provide a basis for comparison as you measure your own clothes.

- Man's Suit/Sportcoat....40 to 42 inches
- Man's Shirt....39 inches
- Man's or Woman's Slacks...26 inches (folded over a hanger)
- Man's or Woman's Slacks....46 inches (hanging from cuffs)
- Woman's Blouse....30 to 34 inches
- Woman's Suit Skirt....34 inches (street length)
- Woman's Dress Skirt....38 inches
- Woman's Blazer/Suit Jacket....32 to 34 inches
- Dresses....45 to 50 inches

Fashions with extremely short or long tails are the exception to these averages. They should not take precedence over the majority of your clothes.

Your final inventory of clothing and accessories, combined with the length in inches of your garments, will now guide you in choosing the best method of storage.

The clothes rod in your closet must be used first for clothes that have to hang, since these garments have no alternative storage space. The first designation to make in your closet is providing sufficient rod space for your hanging clothes. After that obligation has been met, you can turn to the storage of your other clothes (the ones that don't need to hang) and then to the accessories.

As you scrutinize your inventory chart, you may decide to install more rods or you may realize that more shelf space than hanging space is actually required. The inventory makes you aware of your exact needs. Most of your closet space goes to either rods or shelf space. Your closet may end up being an artful blend of both.

Although the inventory has given us a quantity, a question still arises concerning how many horizontal inches of hanging space are needed for the garments you own. As a general rule, if you follow the number of inches allotted below, your garments will be evenly spaced along the rod in an orderly manner and without any crowding or cramming.

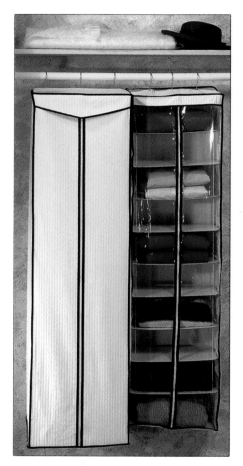

Hanging sweater storage bags are an option for individuals with surplus space.

- Allow one inch of horizontal space per garment.
- Allow two to three inches of horizontal space for each suit, sportcoat, and blazer or jacket, depending on the bulk of the shoulder padding.

Based on these allocations, when categories of clothes are hung together, the computation for the entire group might resemble something like the following:

- 12 skirts occupy 12 inches of horizontal space
- 3 suits occupy six to nine inches of horizontal space

Take a close look at the various closet designs presented in this book. They clearly show an even and orderly spacing for every hanging garment. You can obtain the same attractive appearance and fingertip convenience in your own closet.

You can further enhance the appearance and convenience of the clothes hanging in your closet by employing two simple techniques. First, separate your clothing into distinct categories. Even if you have one long expanse of rod instead of many smaller rod sections, position your garments along the rod by category: slacks together, blouses together, skirts together, and so on. Once each category is hung, arrange the items in each category by color. Begin with the whites and work through the colors from lightest to darkest, until the last garments hanging in that particular category are the blacks.

Arranging your clothes by category and color increases your ability to see and select every garment, which automatically promotes versatility. You'll be able to combine outfits you hadn't realized were complementary. Also, future expenditures on clothes will be more efficient. Once you realize what you actually own, you will tend to buy new articles that coordinate with your existing wardrobe. You'll also be less likely to make an impulsive bargain purchase because you will know you already own three similar garments.

One final routine for your hanging clothes will help prevent clutter sneaking back into your closet: A portion of your clothes rod should be the "workspace" section. This workspace is nothing more than an area designated and left empty for "clothes-in-process."

Dry cleaning, both incoming and outgoing, will occupy this rod space until it is either taken to the cleaners or, for returned cleaning, incorporated back into its proper position within each category. This will help you maintain an orderly environment at all times. Workspace can also be used for those garments that need your attention, such as those with a loose seam, a missing button, or minor wrinkling.

SOME REMINDERS

Keep the following points in mind as you begin formulating tentative plans for designing and arranging your closet space.

- The belongings inside the closet deserve as much thought as the size and shape of the closet.
- Use caution when assigning placement. The initial choice affects all subsequent choices

since it diminishes the amount of space available at later stages of the process.

- Always deliberate before purchasing any product. The product may not always provide the service you desire, and it can sometimes be so awkward and cumbersome to operate that you end up not using it at all.
- When developing your plan, keep similar items grouped together and choose the area of the closet that is most convenient for them. It is easier to look in one location for your shoes or sweaters, instead of having the items scattered throughout your closet.

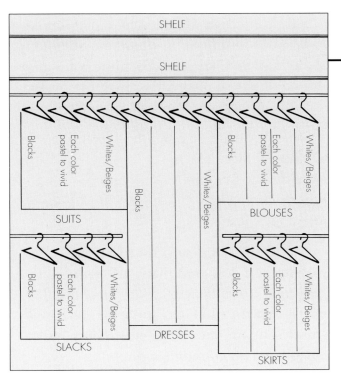

Don't just organize your clothes by category. Within each category, organize the items by color: blacks at one end, whites at the other, and the lighter to darker colors in between.

CHAPTER 3

CLOSET

SYSTEMS

T here are basically five types of closet systems to choose from. Each system offers different varieties, sizes, and qualities of materials, all of which ultimately affect the overall cost of the system. The basic five systems are:

- Separate Shelf/Separate Rod Systems
- Modular Systems
- Ventilated Systems
- Prepackaged Kits
- Instant Closets

While the estimated cost to renovate your closet is certainly important, it's essential to give each closet system an objective evaluation. Then the final decision won't be based strictly on cost but on the entire system's advantages and disadvantages.

The first step in organization is deciding on the type of closet system you will use.

SEPARATE SHELF/SEPARATE ROD SYSTEMS

This is the traditional style of closet, typically seen in most older homes where the closet hasn't already been renovated. Both the shelf (or shelves) and the closet rod are usually either metal or wood, although combinations are fairly common.

The shelf is supported on each side wall and along the back wall by strips of wood that are nailed to the studs of the walls. The shelf itself isn't permanently attached; it can be lifted off the wood strips and removed. The rod is either separate from or fused with the hardware, which is attached to strips of wood installed on the side walls. When these wood strips are removed, holes are left in the wall.

Advantages. Since no extra amenities, such as racks for shoes, ties, or belts, are included or programmed into the structure, you have the freedom to place them where you want rather than where a manufacturer has placed them.

Disadvantages. At least a small degree of carpentry skill is required. The system must be installed between two supporting walls, greatly reducing its versatility.

Costs. The cost of this system depends almost entirely on the quality of the wood you use. This system is usually comparably priced to a ventilated system and costs approximately one-third to one-fourth less than even the cheapest prepackaged modular system. Designing, purchasing, and installing the components yourself will cut the cost by almost half.

MODULAR SYSTEMS

Modular systems consist of presized cubicles and shelves, with structural dividers giving more definition to the closet space. They are still, in essence, a separate shelf/separate rod system but with an upscale appearance.

Unless they are wood, modular systems are made from laminated particle board. The surfaces are usually white, beige, black, or a choice of simulated woods. The closet rod is usually either wood or metal. Sometimes, a plastic-coated color metal rod is offered.

Advantages. These systems look terrific! When modular systems can be modified or custom-designed to your own specifications, they are definitely a top contender. Some of these systems have been refined to such an extent that the volume of available features for storing your accessories is astonishing. The attractiveness adds beauty to your closet. And, on the more practical side, they are the ultimate in attaining "a place for everything and everything in its place."

Disadvantages. The structural dividers eat into your closet's space, reducing the actual space you have available for storing your belongings. This is a problem when you have a smaller closet where every inch counts. The

Modular systems provide shelves and storage cubes. The system below has been colorfully detailed for a contemporary look.

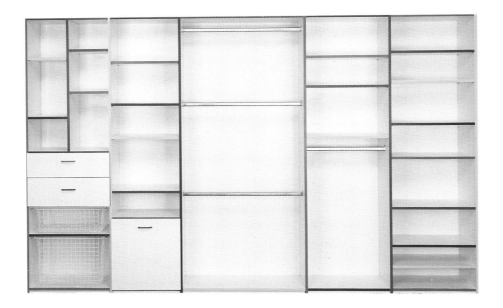

preconstructed modular systems offer only a limited number of sizes and shapes, forcing you to accept someone else's concept of where things should be placed in your closet. These systems seldom match up exactly with your individual needs. Adapting this system to closets that are particularly small or oddly shaped will be especially difficult, if not impossible.

Costs. The quality of the materials used, as well as the number of "specialty" features you choose, will cause great fluctuations in price, ranging from affordable to extravagant. Cost is also affected by the amount of personal participation you are willing or able to give to the project. Certainly, the more you do on the project, such as assembling units yourself or improvising the "specialties" from existing materials you have on hand, the more you save.

VENTILATED SYSTEMS

Although these systems have been around for quite some time, they are still the newest type of closet material. The systems are constructed from metal rods covered with a vinyl or epoxy chip-resistant coating. The diameter of the rod inside the coating is the most important factor to consider: The smaller it is, the less sturdy and dependable the system will be. Take your time investigating the hardware used for installing these systems; some of it isn't reliable. Purchase only those systems with the attached wall "anchor," not the ones that only supply an unsheathed screw. Precise measurements are a must, and a bit of know-how in handling a drill is helpful when installing this system.

Advantages. Ventilated systems are unique in that the overhanging front edge actually becomes the closet rod, extending a mere two inches below the shelf itself. All other closet systems require at least four inches, and sometimes six inches, for the same service. This is due to the thickness of the shelf (¾ inch to 1 inch), the diameter of the rod (1 inch to 2 inches), and the space between the

Ventilated systems work efficiently in odd, hard-to-fit spaces such as this utility area below the basement stairs.

shelf and the rod for hanger access to the rod (2 inches to 3 inches).

Ventilated systems allow the corner area of your closet to hold hanging garments, something no other system can do. Typically, the corner is wasted space. A ventilated system needs no supporting wall at each end for installation; therefore, it can be placed anywhere as a "freestanding" unit. These systems can resolve the problems presented by unusual wall configurations that otherwise would just be wasted space.

There is also a "track system" variation offered in the ventilated line. This allows the height of the shelves to be adjusted easily. For the best all-around service, ventilated systems provide a versatile, adaptable, adjustable, and space-conscious system.

Shelves in a ventilated system promote visibility and help alleviate clutter. Corners, which are usually wasted, also become useful.

Disadvantages. Ventilated systems have vertical struts built into the front edge every 12 inches for added stability. These struts prohibit sliding your hangers the full length of the clothes rod. However, if your closet is properly organized, there should be no reason to shove the hangers aside. Ventilated systems need support braces every 12 inches to 24 inches, and these also prohibit sliding your hangers the length of the rod. Newer versions have corrected this problem by redesigning the brace so it is secured at the top of the shelf, leaving the rod area clear.

Costs. The cost of this system is comparable with that of the separate shelf/separate rod system. Some are available in discount department stores as a prepackaged deal; the quality generally suffers, so test the system for durability and strength of materials and hardware.

PREPACKAGED KITS

These kits actually come in a box containing the necessary pieces to assemble a ventilated system yourself. You won't have to purchase the assorted materials. These kits include an instruction sheet and the necessary hardware.

Advantages. If you do find a kit that fits your specific needs, it's certainly less trouble to carry home just one box.

Disadvantages. There are a limited number of possible configurations, restricting the number of possible designs. You might see an unassembled kit designed precisely as you would like your own finished closet to be, but that kit may not be suitable for your closet's size and shape. You're lucky when all the pieces fit and disappointed when they don't.

Costs. Unless they're on sale, prepackaged kits seldom cost any less than buying the components separately. In fact, kits can cost a bit more because you're paying for precut lengths.

CHAPTER 4

HANGERS

AND
OTHER EQUIPMENT

K eep wire hangers out of your closet! They are constantly becoming tangled because their necks are too small and narrow. Wire hangers are dirty, and they snag and damage clothing. They easily fall off the clothes rod, creating clutter on the floor. And, they seem to multiply once the closet door is closed and the light turned off.

Simply switching from wire hangers to any one of the many alternative styles available will add uniformity and appeal to your closet. But don't be hasty. Some hangers perform their duty far better than others by implementing helpful features. Other hangers actu-

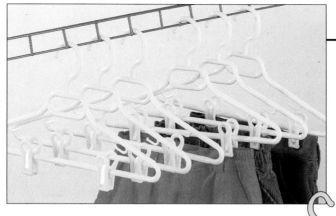

Plastic tubular hangers are a popular choice for hanging clothes.

ally hinder the smooth functioning of a closet's performance by becoming snarled on the closet rod.

The plastic tubular hanger is usually the first alternative hanger to be considered. It's easily available and inexpensive, and it comes in a wide range of colors for decorative coordinating. But it only furnishes the single function of hanging clothes. Many varieties of plastic hangers are inferior in quality, and they break, bend, or sag. Purchase only the sturdier, thicker models. Many of these hangers include "notches," but the vast majority of these notched hangers are flawed. Whenever the thin shoulder straps or the hanging loops inside the waistband of a skirt are put in the notch, they usually slip and slide out.

Another type of hanger, called an attachable hanger, can be used to take advantage of the amazing amount of usable space that is wasted in a traditional layout. Typically, a closet rod runs the length of the closet and your clothes are hung on this rod. If you look to the bottom edge of these hanging garments, however, you will see an invitingly empty area. At least a third of the hangers from the rod could be removed and repositioned in this vacant space using attachables. Attachable hangers are also known as add-ons because they have an extra hook in the center that allows other hangers to be attached to the one above. Clothes can be aligned vertically in the closet rather than horizontally across the closet rod.

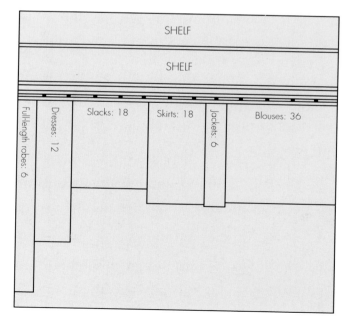

This vertical arrangement, called layering, enables you to hang two to eight garments, yet the closet rod holds only one hanger. This is perhaps the single most effective organizing technique you can initiate. It's also the most economical in terms of time, energy, and money.

Attachable hangers present other advantages as well. Hanging garments aren't crammed together on the clothes rod, so wrinkles are minimized. Also, clothes are not shoved from one side of the closet rod to another when searching for and retrieving an item. By arranging each layer in its proper color sequence, a system for maintaining order is automatically established. When a

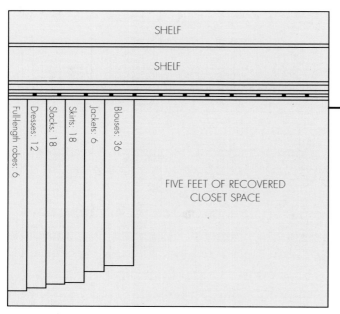

SHELF

SHELF

Full-length robes: 6

Dresses: 12

Slacks: 18

Skirts: 18

Jackets: 6

Blouses: 36

FIVE FEET OF RECOVERED CLOSET SPACE

These design plans demonstrate how using attachable hangers to keep categories of clothes together can greatly increase storage capacity.

garment is replaced, you need not insert it between garments in the layer. Instead, merely hang it at the bottom of the color-arranged row, and it will recycle itself.

The best advantage of all is the extra space you gain when you use attachable hangers. By changing from standard (wire or plastic) hangers to attachable hangers, your closet's hanging capacity can be greatly increased. If additional hanging space isn't essential, consider this: Using attachable hangers opens up space for shelves, cubby-holes, drawer units, or other storage devices you might be wishing you could allocate space for.

Attachable hangers also come in a variation for hanging skirts. These skirt hangers do a superb job with strapless dresses, silky undergarments, and shorts, and they never lose their hold.

Another style of hanger that is useful is the open-end slacks hanger. These hangers pack a mighty wallop in gaining control of your closet space. Slacks slide on and off the unencumbered opening of the hanger without the bother of removing the hanger from the rod. The neck is bigger and rounder than most any other type of hanger, so it won't snarl or snag with

Attachable hangers have hooks in the center that can hold other hangers.

the other hangers on the rod. These hangers are also smaller in stature, being three to four inches shorter in length and width. The smaller size opens up areas of the closet where a standard-size hanger cannot go. This provides better use of space, allowing for more innovative and creative designs.

Yet another style of hanger serves a dual purpose, combining the two pieces of an ensemble. However, this hanger requires more vertical space since it hangs the skirt or slacks at least four inches lower than other types of hangers. Also, by hanging matched sets of clothes on one hanger, a great deal of versatility is hidden, which limits their wearability. People have a tendency to wear the set as one unit. If the two separate pieces are hung on two separate hangers, the hangers used can be more suitable to the particular garment they are carrying. The jacket of a suit, for instance, would hang with the other jackets on the rod above the skirts and slacks. It then becomes possible to combine that jacket with other coordinated or complementary bottoms. The same holds true when the skirt of the suit is placed with the other skirts.

SYSTEMS FOR ACCESSORIES

When organizing a closet, one objective is to store each classification of accessories effec-

Drawer organizers divide larger spaces into smaller, more manageable ones.

tively and efficiently. If each group of accessories was handled independently, each group could be stored in the least amount of space, with maximum accessibility and visibility. But all your accessories must be dealt with at once: You need to find a method of storage for your shoes, sweaters, belts, neckties, handbags, and jewelry that is compatible and efficient for all accessories. This is known as maximized space utilization. For example, if you have an arrangement of modular shelf/drawer units, storage capacity can be nearly doubled by inserting additional shelves between the existing shelves. At the same time, the length, depth, and height of the storage unit itself is unchanged, occupying the same amount of floor space and wall space. This same idea can be applied to any closet in your house.

Dividing larger spaces into smaller, more manageable segments that more closely resemble the size and shape of the items they hold eliminates the stacks and piles of garments and accessories that are so common in closets. Drawer organizers work well for positioning and arranging articles in a drawer so that each article is plainly visible. Regarding shelf storage, acrylic shelf dividers provide an adaptable and easy yet efficient way to segregate a whole shelf into specifically assigned storage compartments. These dividers are perfect for handbags, sweaters, hats, or any other conceivable item.

Remember, with any storage system it is important to choose only those storage methods that are easy to use and become second nature. This does not mean that the product

Shelf dividers keep items upright, visible, and prevent disastrous pile-ups.

or hardware should be a simple design but that the method of storage should be appropriate for your belongings. If your method does not coincide with your own routine usage, your closet will soon be in disorder and disarray again no matter how well-intentioned or disciplined you are.

For example, a plain two-inch hook is about as simple a piece of hardware as can be found. And screwing a row of hooks into a wall of your closet for hanging belts, ties, and scarves is an easy method of storage. But difficulties will arise when two, three, or more items are hung on the same hook. You then have to search and remove all the items to retrieve the one you want. In this case, the method that will guarantee smooth and unencumbered efficiency is to hang only one article on each hook.

After deciding where your hanging clothes will be accommodated inside your closet (but before you actually hang those items), you should consider what to do with the smaller sections of space that will hold your accessories. These smaller areas are the shelves, the floor, the side walls, and the wall space above and to each side of the closet door. Sweaters and shoes are the two main contenders for most of this remaining space; the methods for storing shoes are more flexible, compact, and innovative.

SHOE STORAGE

The over-the-door shoe rack was discussed earlier, and it resolves shoe storage in a practical, space-saving manner. This type of shoe rack will often work effectively on sliding doors as long as it is installed on the inside surface of the innermost door. This rack can also be hung on the back wall of the closet (behind the hanging clothes) or on the side wall of the closet (if you can spare five inches of clearance).

This basic idea was streamlined and its versatility improved by reducing the rack to a

A boot rack is a good addition near a back door to avoid tracking wet, dirty shoe stains inside your home.

single compact strip that can fit in even the tightest wall space. You can arrange one, two, or more strips in whatever configuration suits the wall space and the number of shoes to be stored. Several strips of this shoe storage rack can hold many more shoes than other, more traditional methods of storage.

The simple molded plastic floor rack for shoe storage has probably been purchased more than any other type of shoe storage rack. But most of the time it is left sitting on the floor unused, with shoes in heaps around it. Even more distressing, its existence prevents you from doubling the hanging capacity in your closet because it occupies the space where a second, lower closet rod could be installed. And these racks don't store shoes in the least amount of space. But, if the only excess space you have is on the floor, look for the rack that will best fit your shoe or boot styles.

If you kept your shoes in their cardboard boxes or in transparent shoe boxes on the shelf or floor, the shoes occupy less space. The secret for the successful application of this method lies in how the boxes are stacked, aligned, and combined. If the stacks are more than 3 or 4 boxes high, the system will be too awkward to handle. The exception is with a self-supporting system of shoe boxes that has a structure surrounding the boxes. With this system, the boxes can be slid in and out with-

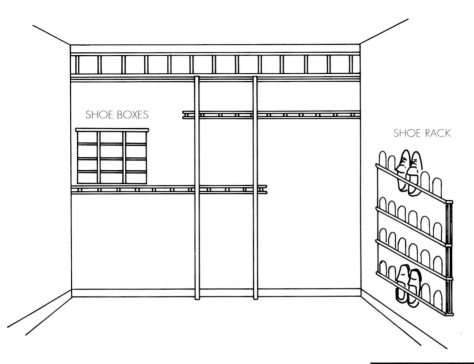

SHOE BOXES

SHOE RACK

out disturbing the other boxes. Keeping like styles stored in close proximity, once again, encourages routine. For example, store sandals by other sandals and boots in their own area. As we have discussed throughout this publication, that is the goal.

Consider your own set of variables—the space available for shoe storage and the number of shoes you must store—and keep the following guidelines in mind.

- First, target the places in your closet that are unused and unproductive. These areas can usually handle shoe storage well and can't

If your closet cannot hold all your shoes in one area, store shoes in different areas.

handle other items, such as sweaters. Don't use rod space for shoe storage, even if you own a perfectly dandy shoe bag designed for the clothes rod. This consumes rod space, better used for hanging clothes, which could lead to piles of clutter from lack of space. Exactly what you were trying to alleviate from the start.

- Never use more space than necessary, unless the system is so efficient it warrants extra space or your closet is so spacious it can afford the luxury. Never choose a system based only on its beauty or uniqueness. Practicality and need should be your first and foremost guides.

- Allow a little extra room for new acquisitions. Sometimes you must recognize that you don't have enough space in any one area of the closet to store every pair of shoes you already own. In that case, divide your shoes into separate categories, such as casual, sporty,

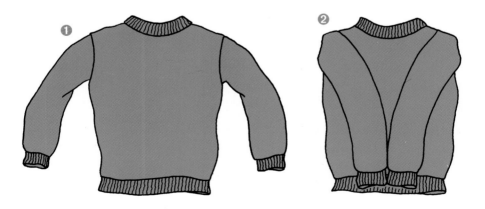

dressy, and the like, and select spots that will accommodate these smaller groupings. Another alternative is to get rid of an old pair of shoes or boots if you purchase a new pair.

SWEATER STORAGE

Because of their bulk, sweaters are by far the most confusing and complex accessory to store. It is inadvisable to lump all your sweaters together into one category because sweaters serve many purposes from warmth to fashion. Sweaters can be for outerwear or innerwear, dressy, casual, turtleneck, beaded, appliquéd, or embossed. With so many sweaters, it can be difficult to find the one you want. Instead, you may just end up wearing the first one you en-counter as you search through your drawers and shelves. Most people have grown accus-tomed to the familiar ritual of retrieving, refold-

To roll a sweater:
❶ Lay the sweater front side down (except V-necks). ❷ Fold the arms and a small section of each side so the sweater is only 12 inches wide. ❸ Flip up ⅓ of the bottom and start rolling at this fold. ❹ The result is a smooth-ly rolled knit.

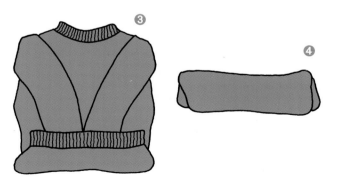

ing, and restacking sweaters and have concluded that any storage method for sweaters is too bothersome.

The majority of people fall into three groups when it comes to storing sweaters. The first group stuffs their sweaters into drawers or sliding wire baskets. Next is the group that never gives sweater storage a thought, and they hang sweaters in the closet or keep them in bags on the bottom of the closet. The last group will carefully fold their sweaters and then pile them on the closet shelf. If you use any of these methods, pay close attention to the following discussion.

Drawers, no matter how diverse or where located, furnish the poorest visibility and accessibility to sweaters of any method. If drawers are your only recourse for sweater storage, roll the sweaters rather than fold them. Place the rolled edge up and align the sweaters in the drawer single file from

Hangers made specifically for knits reduce "hanger-burn," but they do not store sweaters as well as rolling.

Another way to store your sweaters for maximum visibility is on a shelf with transparent doors.

front to back or side to side. Now each sweater is visible and handy.

Delicate knitted garments can easily suffer "hanger-burn" if they are hung as though they were just another blouse. Even if you hang sweaters on a hanger made especially for knits, wrinkles, puckers, and creases will soon appear, although the wrinkles and creases are minor compared with hanger-burns.

There's nothing wrong with positioning stacks of sweaters on a shelf in your closet, but ways exist to improve this method by preventing the stacks from toppling over and keeping the stacks neat. Earlier, it was mentioned that dividing shelf space into smaller, more manageable sections works well for storage. A system for doing this involves using acrylic shelf dividers. There are styles, shapes, and sizes of shelf dividers on the market to suit anyone's taste and budget: inexpensive plastic stackable shelves; laminated modular shelf units; vertical dividers that attach to existing shelves, and boxes with a zippered or flip-front opening. Any of these shelving styles can be positioned on the shelf to create the desired compartments. They can also be stacked and combined on the floor of the closet, creating a wall unit for storage. Putting sweaters in sweater boxes, sweater bags, or zippered sweater cases will not provide the high level of performance you are striving for. A system of plastic bins placed on the shelf is inadvisable because it functions in the same manner as a drawer and presents the same disadvantages.

Belts and ties can be stored on the same rack (right). Some racks roll out from the wall and have a separate hook for each tie or belt (above).

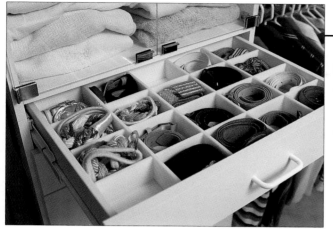

Belts also can be rolled up and placed in individual drawer dividers.

BELT, TIE, AND JEWELRY RACKS

A belt ring muddles belts together. Equipping your closet with one will cause the same frustration as a simple nail in the wall holding numerous belts. A belt ring has another negative attribute in that it occupies space on the closet rod. Rod space should hold only hanging garments with no exceptions. Any style of belt rack that provides an ample number of hooks for the placement of individual belts and that can be installed on the side or back walls of your closet is the best type of rack for belts.

Many tie racks actually make ties inaccessible and are designed to hang from the closet rod. Many of the ties will be too well concealed from sight. To get to those ties, you'll have to maneuver through a large portion of ties you don't intend to wear. Just like the belt rack, a style of tie rack with hooks that can be installed on a closet wall for each individual tie is the best type of tie rack to use. With some of these tie racks, by extending the arms outward for easy selection and access, you can see the full complement of ties. Afterward, the arms fold back into the unit, and the unit slides back into its original position. This applies to scarves as well as ties. Placing the tie rack close to your dress shirts is another habit-reinforcement trick.

The biggest mistake regarding jewelry is thinking that it's OK to store it in your dresser

Modular jewelry boxes placed in drawers help prevent clutter.

drawers. It doesn't make sense to keep delicate rings and necklaces in a large drawer without protection. Also, jewelry should not be kept in the same drawer with hairbrushes, cameras, pencils, and the like. A good idea is to assign a jewelry drawer. This drawer should not be handled like a junk drawer.

Jewelry requires containers that are scaled to their size; jewelry boxes, bags, pouches, chests, and cases meet this requirement with varying degrees of success.

Also, jewelry should not be treated as a single category. Necklaces, for instance, are far better served from a hanging position rather than stashed helter skelter in a drawer, even if the drawer is in a jewelry box. Just about any sort of gadget or rack for hanging necklaces systematically will serve your purpose. As with the storage of other items, placing your jewelry in transparent containers is always beneficial. The increased visibility saves time, since the contents of each container can be seen immediately. There will be no more searching through all your jewelry boxes looking for the one item you want.

CHAPTER 5

CLOSET
CONFIGURATIONS

So far, the discussion has focused on the
fundamentals you need to begin the drawings
for your closet design. While reading, you have
probably been accepting and rejecting certain
aspects of the information presented, which is
fine. You need to take the information and use
it to fit your needs and evaluate what you'd
like from your closets. With this information,
the drawings themselves will flow smoothly
with less trial and error. Remember, though,
that the first drawing is seldom perfect; it is
difficult for most people to visualize all the
components without setting them to paper.

It would be foolish to begin the physical
manipulation of your closet without progress-
ing through the design stage. This stage of the

process assures that the pieces of the plan fit together aesthetically, that the plan is structurally feasible, and that the space permits the items you plan to use. This prevents the unpleasant surprises or costly mistakes that are bound to occur should you bypass the design stage. And often, as you draw the initial design, you may notice something that was overlooked or you may be able to improve on an idea. This makes the finished product more satisfactory.

To visualize the perspectives of your closet, which will help show items in the closet in relation to each other, you will need to draw two kinds of diagrams to represent your closet space. These are the "bird's-eye view" and the "dead-ahead view." The dead-ahead view is typically illustrated in photographs and sketches. Unfortunately, this view doesn't adequately portray

By starting with a thought-out design plan, you can set up an orderly closet in your home, and keep it that way! This his and her closet suits the needs of both people.

Two diagrams–the bird's-eye view (top) and the dead-ahead view (bottom)–will help you visualize the space in your closet.

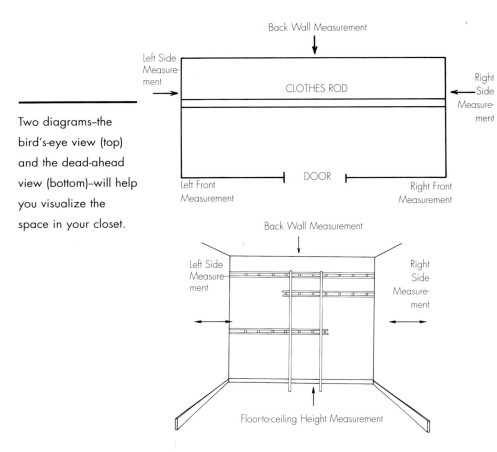

the interaction inside the closet between the materials (rods, shelves, racks) and your garments and accessories. A bird's-eye view—the vantage point from the ceiling—solves this problem. Combining both views, all visual aspects of your closet are projected, filling in the gaps left by each view independently.

For instance, in a bird's-eye view you merely see the diameter and width of the closet rod. Your garments are what actually take up space, not the rod. As another example, your clothes rods may be installed on each side wall of your closet. Examine how this affects any remaining space on those side walls. You may inadvertently discount this space because of the rods and thus lose any remaining usable space on those walls. Or, you may try to use the whole wall even though you only have smaller sections of space around the rods to work with.

USE EVERY INCH

Remember, you want to profit from every available inch of space in your closet. People tend to mismanage readily available space, using it as a huge lost and found. Often, assorted possessions are simply pitched up to the top shelf, and the shelf becomes an example of "out-of-sight, out-of-mind." This top shelf area enables you to double or triple your storage capacity; you'll only need to incorporate a step stool into the closet design. Once the step stool is in place, you must use it or you'll find yourself pitching items to the top shelf all over again.

Note the illustration on page 64 of a rather typically designed wall closet (minus the closet doors). A great deal of usable space is being wasted, both above the top shelf and below the hanging clothes. But you will need hanging space, shelf space, or ideally a beneficial blend of both. The characteristics of your clothing and accessories may designate the need for more shelves rather than more hanging capacity. Additional illustrations on the next page explore two different directions you could take to achieve this objective. Keep in mind that these illustrations are simplified depictions. They are not the fully developed drawings you'll need as a final diagram of your closet space, which would include storage racks and containers. Those finishing touches come later.

A typically designed closet has one shelf and one rod; it does not use space very efficiently.

One of the following sample closet designs may resemble your own closet. This discussion will concentrate on the details: Why store an accessory in a certain manner and location? Some techniques that are portrayed are applicable to all closets. In each illustration, a new and different technique will be highlighted. These illustrations will show you how to go about the process of committing your closet's measurements to paper, as well as how to sketch in the specific pertinent information you've been gathering along the way. It's time to put all of that information together in the form of a diagram that places your garments and accessories in a drawing of your closet.

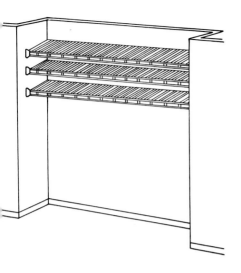

THE FRONT-TO-BACK CLOSET

Previously, only the "side wall to side wall" type has been discussed because not all closets can accommodate the alternative approach called the front-to-back closet. This creates a closet that maximizes space, while furnishing convenience and accessibility.

Your own closet must meet certain requirements if you wish to effectively use this alternative design. Consider the position of the door in relation to the space on each side of the door. If the closet door is nearly flush to a side wall, providing little recessed depth, a front-to-back transformation can't be installed because the hanging clothing would intrude into the entrance of the closet. If there is a recessed

These illustrations depict two ways to redesign a closet to achieve more storage space. Add more shelves (left) or add shelves and an extra hanging rod (right).

depth on one or both sides, you must decide whether to use both or only one. On the other hand, if the depth of the recessed wall is excessive, a front-to-back installation might decrease the closet's capacity.

Also consider the front-to-back depth of the closet. If this depth is meager, there may not be sufficient space to warrant this approach. In other words, if you gain no advantage by turning the clothes perpendicular to normal, there's little reason to pursue this alternative.

Make an exact drawing of the side-to-side system; include a count of the actual number of garments and accessories that can be handled with this design. Then make an exact drawing of the front-to-back system, again including the tally of articles this method could store. Draw the bird's-eye view of each. Thoroughly evaluate the drawings for each system, comparing positive and negative elements. This procedure will make you aware of the consequences, advantages, and compromises you're making.

STANDARD WALL CLOSET: 42 INCHES WIDE

This is just about the smallest clothes closet anyone is likely to have. Saving space here is very important. The shoes are placed on a shoe rack on the left side wall because of the door's position. This shoe storage method requires only five inches of space to operate efficiently. The racks for ties, belts, and scarves are placed on the opposite side wall. Since the racks are at the same heights as the ventilated shelving, there is sufficient space for the lengths of the belts. The boots are hung from the ceiling, but not directly in front of the shelf. You may hang as many pairs as you like as long as they don't block access to the shelves. Placing the boots on the ceiling stores them without using any storage space. The cubbyholes on

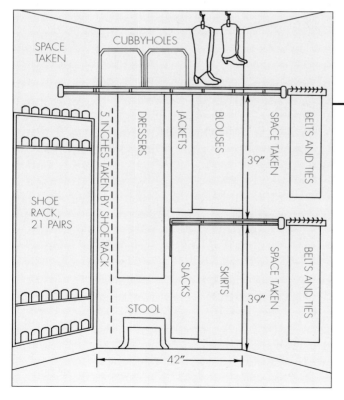

This design illustrates one way to get the most out of a small 42-inch-wide closet.

the shelf, for purses or sweaters, could be substituted for other kinds of shelf dividers. The main idea is to divide the height and length of the ventilated shelf into smaller compartments. Using attachable, or add-on, hangers increases the number of garments the closet can hold (from about 58 to about 99). A step stool is also a permanent fixture in this closet, otherwise the boots and top shelf would be out of reach. The diagram also indicates where space is being occupied ("space taken" in the illustration). Space is no longer available in those areas because of the placement of items on the adjoining wall.

STANDARD WALL CLOSET: 100 INCHES WIDE

This design provides some alternatives to the smaller 42-inch closet. The primary objective of the first design is to provide maximum hanging capabilities. But the 100-inch-wide closet manages to incorporate an extra six feet of shelf space, in addition to the full-length top shelf, by adding cubbyholes in a vertical alignment. Only 12 inches of hanging space were exchanged for this extra shelf space. The ventilated system allows the lower shelf and rod to stand free. With a modular system, a supporting wall would be needed.

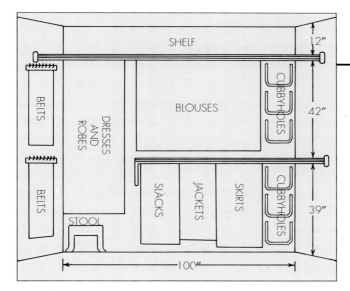

Diagram labels:

SHELF

12"

BELTS

BLOUSES

CUBBYHOLES

42"

DRESSES AND ROBES

BELTS

SLACKS

JACKETS

SKIRTS

CUBBYHOLES

39"

STOOL

100"

This 100-inch-wide closet offers many more options for organizing than the smaller 42-inch-wide closet.

STANDARD WALL CLOSET: 106 INCHES WIDE

This larger closet can be designed quite differently from the previous two closets: The main focus is to promote a harmonious combination of hanging space and shelf space. Although this closet seems to be the same as the 100-inch-wide closet, there is a major difference. This closet has space on the wall that also holds the closet door. This provides 24 inches of additional space on each side of the closet. The potential for effective organization is greatly enhanced because of this extra space. The front-to-back method could be used on either or both sides of the closet. The 24-inch wall located on each side of the door could

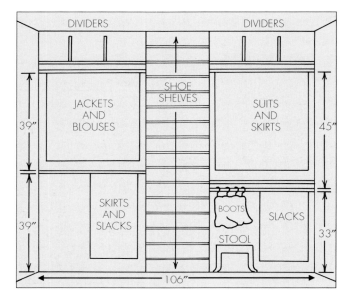

Diagram labels:

DIVIDERS | DIVIDERS

JACKETS AND BLOUSES — 39"

SHOE SHELVES

SUITS AND SKIRTS — 45"

SKIRTS AND SLACKS — 39"

BOOTS

SLACKS — 33"

STOOL

106"

Shelves and dividers are used effectively in this illustration.

contain shoe racks or belt/tie racks without any reduction in visibility or accessibility.

THE WALK-IN CLOSET

Many people are more intimi-dated by the designing of a walk-in closet than a standard wall closet, but the only difference is that you draw more than one wall for a complete design. Only one thing can cause failure: Not understanding how each piece comes together in the corners of the closet. When the rods and shelves of two walls butt into each other in the corner, that corner space can be functional in only one direction. The main advantage of a walk-in closet over a standard wall closet is the walk-in closet's capability to keep each closet function separate from the others. One entire wall can be used for hanging, and another entire wall can be used for shelving. The standard wall closet must combine hanging and shelving on the same wall. In addition, walk-in closets offer so

much increased wall space that it is seldom
necessary to conserve space to the same degree
as in a standard wall closet.

The illustrations below show configurations of walk-in closets. Take time to review
them to see if they resemble your own.

The small "inset" walls, shorter walls, or
the inside surface of the doors supply the perfect spot for belt/tie racks or wall shoe racks. A
closet with a door that opens inward and is
flush with the side wall prevents use of part of
the wall for any major closet component.

A walk-in closet offers
the option to use one
entire wall for shelves
or clothes rods (below
left). If the door is flush
to a side wall, the best
use for this space is
mirrors (below).

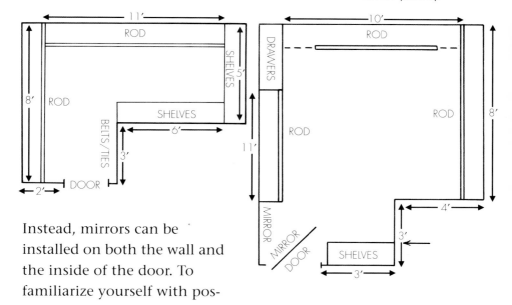

Instead, mirrors can be
installed on both the wall and
the inside of the door. To
familiarize yourself with pos-
sible designs for a walk-in closet, use three
separate sets of drawings. Break the walls of
your closet into those intended for hanging
clothes, those designed for shelving, and those

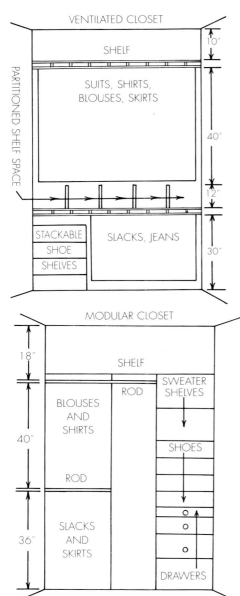

meant for combining both functions. Each drawing should specify the total amount of storage space obtained from each wall using a particular design. This will give you a better basis for evaluating effective space use.

The illustrations on this page depict various ways to organize each wall of a walk-in closet. Shorter widths are given in the designs because it is generally easier to stretch a small diagram than to fit a large design into a smaller space. The heights of the closet rods and shelves may need to be altered based on your individual preferences.

ODD AND UNUSUAL CLOSETS

Believe it or not, closets with odd or unusual spaces are easier to design. Since they have short walls, sloping walls, or asymmetric walls, you have fewer options for assigning placement of items. "Normal" closets can handle almost any design suggestion, which can lead to

For a walk-in closet, use rods only (top). Or, combine rods, shelves, and drawers in a modular system (bottom).

impulsive decisions that could adversely affect the design. But the heights and shapes of the walls in an odd closet predetermine what service they can perform. For example, longer garments like dresses and robes can't hang from walls that are only 18 inches to 24 inches high. The reverse is also true; you don't want to hang slacks—the shortest garment in your wardrobe—from a section of wall space that is eight feet high. Although your design options are fairly cut-and-dried compared with the designs for a standard or walk-in closet, a great many helpful ideas are presented in the illustrations on pages 74 and 75.

A closet can have a completely separate storage system placed in its design called an island. This is a freestanding unit that doesn't need any other part of the closet for installation. It furnishes a significant amount of storage space while leaving the rest of the closet available for storage.

Play with different structural dimensions as well as various interior arrangements while designing the layout of your island. But keep your primary objectives in mind and establish priorities before you begin. Ask yourself several questions: What articles of clothing and accessories are most suitable to this form of storage? Can you fit a complete category (all sweaters, all shoes) into the island or will the island permit only a partial collection? If you can store an entire category, is that the smartest course of action, considering the shelf space still available in the rest of the closet? How big can the island be? The floor space determines maximum length and depth, and the sloping walls will dictate height.

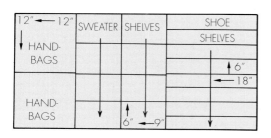

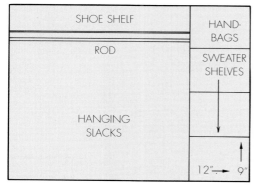

The back of the one-foot-deep island can fit a pegboard for ties (top). The front and back of the two-feet-deep island can hold slacks (bottom).

Look at the illustrations on this page depicting two types of islands. One island is 12 inches deep, the other 24 inches deep. The 12-inch-deep island could have a pegboard or system of racks on either the back or the two sides of the unit, creating a place for belts, ties, scarves, and hanging jewelry. The top surface would be handy for folding clothes or for routine handling of clothes and accessories. The 24-inch-deep island allows access from both sides, doubling its storage capacity. This method also provides the best visibility, since nothing sits hidden behind an item at the front of the shelf. The interior shelves can be easily created using cubbyholes or portable stackable shelf units. Building the island itself, however, is definitely a job for a person experienced with lumber, saw, hammer, and nails.

The cubbyhole treatment also works well for the sloping walls of an unusual closet. You can obtain either horizontal (along a shelf) or vertical (hanging from a shelf) configurations. Cubbyholes can also provide storage compartments for low walls encountered in unusual closets. Generally, the sloping wall creates a pyramid-shape space with the shelf space. Don't automatically discount this odd space as useless. By adding a few transparent shoe boxes or sweater drawers, you can turn this area into a plentiful storage compartment.

Odd closets are seldom spacious, so they rarely meet all your needs. A workspace area— to hold dry cleaning, empty hangers, or clothes to be mended—can be implemented by installing a smaller "closet rod." It also provides a place to hang garments you're surveying for potential inclusion in a suitcase.

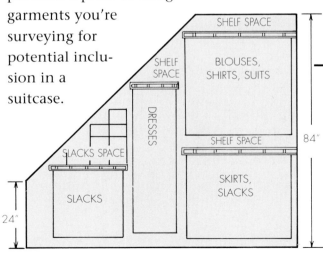

This side view shows yet another design for an unusual closet. Be sure to make use of the pyramid-shape caused by the sloping wall and shelf space.

HIS AND HER
CLOSET

S ince men and women are quite different in appearance, it is not surprising that their clothing and personal accessories are quite different. An exploration of strategies and techniques for closet storage will ensure there is a proper and agreeable division of space in the closet a man and woman share. Some items of clothing and some types of accessories are ordinarily unisex in nature, such as slacks and belts. These items require little, if any, special emphasis or treatment. But there is an impressive array of articles that are distinctly feminine or masculine, and need specific discussion.

A woman's wardrobe usually includes dresses, skirts, shirts, suits, sweaters, dress shoes,

casual shoes, handbags, necklaces, and other jewelry. A man's wardrobe consists of similar items including suits, shirts, ties, jackets, sweaters, and casual wear. The issue becomes more a matter of space than classification, since a man's garments are usually longer than a woman's.

So, how is space in a his and her closet fairly divided? How do you recognize where and when to increase the vertical heights of closet rods and shelf heights? A significant, though subtle, factor is that space can be used more effectively on the man's side of the closet. All his space can be double-rodded since nothing is longer than a suit coat or shirt, and the height

Many design systems are feasible for a his and her closet. Base your choice on the system that best fits your needs.

of the shoe shelves need not extend above the height of his dress shoes or cushioned running shoes. A woman's half of the closet must have sufficient space to hang dresses, as well as shelf space designed to fit high-heel shoes, knee-high boots, or wide-brimmed hats.

A drawer with dividers makes a good choice to store all kinds of jewelry, belts, and hair accessories.

As with any closet project, the first step is to establish a set of standard operational procedures, or handling instructions, for the items that will go in the closet. Do not deviate from these guidelines; without standard procedures, you cannot maintain control of your closet.

Remove accompanying belts from slacks, skirts, and dresses. Otherwise, the garments may be stretched out of shape. Belts belong on a belt rack or rolled up and stored in a drawer with dividers. When hanging slacks, match the inside seam to the outside seam at the bottom edge. Hold the slacks at the bottom, and the crease line is defined. Buttoning or zipping the slacks misaligns the crease. Simply follow the crease line to the waistband and gently mold the zipper and placket into a fold. Then fold the slacks near the middle of their length and insert them onto a hanger, keeping the fold in the center of the hanger. You may prefer to hang your slacks by their full length, which calls for a type of hanger known as a clamp hanger. But be warned: These hangers might mar the cuffs of slacks or the waist-bands of skirts by leaving pressure marks that are difficult to remove.

When hanging blouses, shirts, and dresses, fasten the top button, perhaps the top two, or, best of all, every other button for the entire length of the garment. This eliminates wrinkles, cock-eyed collars, and twisted plackets. Perhaps the worst habit you can get into is deliberately pulling a garment from its hanger. Instead, re-move the hanger from the rod and then unbut-ton the garment from the hanger.

When handbags are placed on a shelf or in a cubbyhole, they should face the same direc-tion and be in an upright position. Create di-vided compartments for handbags, with each compartment containing one color or a range of colors from light to dark. Closures should be properly buckled, snapped, or tied shut; if the straps or handles can be placed inside the handbag, do so.

The primary focus of a his and her closet should be forming a real or imaginary divider between "his" side and "her" side of the closet. But this line shouldn't hinder the overall use-fulness of the closet for either of the partici-pants. This divider can be easily obtained, and there are several approaches to achieving this objective. Perhaps the simplest course is installing a wall in the middle, or near the middle, of the closet. Once a divider has been agreed upon, each separate side of the closet is

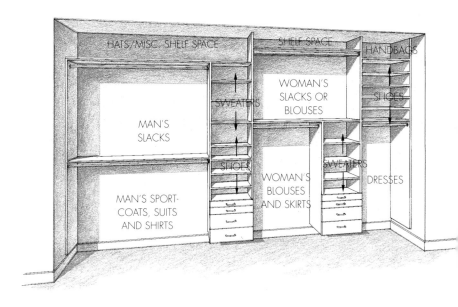

HATS/MISC. SHELF SPACE

SHELF SPACE

HANDBAGS

WOMAN'S SLACKS OR BLOUSES

SWEATERS

SHOES

MAN'S SLACKS

SHOES

MAN'S SPORT-COATS, SUITS AND SHIRTS

WOMAN'S BLOUSES AND SKIRTS

SWEATERS

DRESSES

A smaller version of the his and her closet still allots a good number of drawers, shelves, and rod space.

then treated as a complete and separate entity: a woman's closet and a man's closet.

In the photograph of the his and her closet on page 77, the shelf and drawer unit functions as the central dividing line. However, the woman was favored with a section of space to the right of the drawers and shelves in addition to the entire left side of the closet. This is not uncommon. Women are usually given more space because women usually own more categories of clothing as well as more clothes within each category than men. Keep in mind that you should plan and allocate space based on your own individual needs. If he owns more clothing he will need more space than the woman sharing the closet.

In this closet design, all supports and appointments are kept off the floor. This adds an extra convenience: You can run the vacuum cleaner or dust mop into every corner, reaching every inch where dust collects. Many shelf units available hold sweaters and shoes inside transparent drawer units. Since these type of Lucite drawers are somewhat expensive, not every sweater and pair of shoes can be stored this way. So you might want to use these drawers for the dressier and more costly shoes that are seldom worn.

Each part of your closet can be designed in a variety of configurations. You must determine which aspects of the given designs are most productive and effective for your own situation and circumstances.

WOMAN'S

CLOSET

Y ou may be facing a rough situation in your closet as you begin to organize. It can be a disheartening picture.

First, remove the clothing from the rod and the stacks of merchandise strewn on the shelf and floor. Place these items into groups of similar objects. Calculate how much room you'll need for each group, then measure the space available in the closet—length, width, and depth. You will then have the numbers you need to formulate a tentative layout. This layout is much like working with a group of building blocks of assorted sizes. Give some thought to the items of a woman's wardrobe that must go in these "blocks" of space: dresses, skirts, sweaters, blouses, high heels, casual

shoes, handbags, necklaces, and a range of other items. The closet must have sufficient space to hang the dresses, as well as shelf space designed to fit high-heel shoes, knee-high boots, or hats. After the hanging clothes have been positioned in the layout, play around with your remaining "blocks" of space, both horizontally and vertically, to fill in the gaps with your accessories.

As with any closet project, the route from a disorganized mess to a neat and orderly closet design starts with establishing a set of standard operational procedures, or handling instructions, for the clothes and accessories that will be stored in the closet. Do not deviate from these guidelines; without standard procedures,

Note the categories of this woman's wardrobe: sweaters, shoes, and handbags on shelves; dresses, jackets, and suits combined in sections.

you cannot maintain control of your closet.

Remove accompanying belts from slacks, skirts, and dresses. Otherwise, the garments may be stretched out of shape. Belts belong on a belt rack. When hanging slacks, match the inside seam to the outside seam at the bottom edge. Hold the slacks at the bottom, and the crease line is defined. Buttoning or zipping the slacks misaligns the crease. Simply follow the crease line to the waistband and gently mold the zipper and placket into a fold. Then fold the slacks near the middle of their length and insert them onto a hanger, keeping the fold in the center of the hanger. You may prefer to hang your slacks by their full length, which calls for a type of hanger known as a clamp hanger. But be warned: These hangers might mar the cuffs of slacks or the waistbands of skirts by leaving pressure marks that are difficult to remove.

When hanging blouses and dresses, fasten the top button, perhaps the top two, or, best of all, every other button for the entire length of the garment. This eliminates wrinkles, cock-eyed collars, and twisted plackets. After putting the garment on the hanger, place the hanger on the rod so that all hangers face the same direction. Perhaps the worst habit you can get into is deliberately pulling a garment from its hanger. Instead, remove the hanger and unbutton the garment from the hanger.

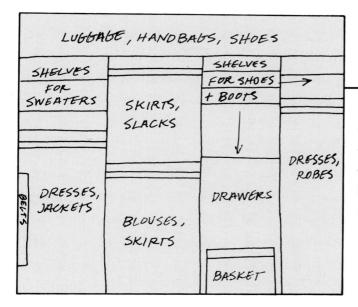

The diagram shows a closet layout with the following labeled sections:

LUGGAGE, HANDBAGS, SHOES

SHELVES FOR SWEATERS

SHELVES FOR SHOES + BOOTS

SKIRTS, SLACKS

DRESSES, ROBES

DRESSES, JACKETS

DRAWERS

BLOUSES, SKIRTS

BASKET

Your closet can be converted into a neat and orderly space by creating a design that breaks your wardrobe into categories.

When handbags are placed on a shelf or in a cubbyhole, they should face the same direction and be in an upright position. Create divided compartments for handbags, with each compartment containing one color or a range of colors from light to dark. Closures should be properly buckled, snapped, or tied shut; if the straps or handles can be placed inside the handbag, do so. This stops the straps from getting tangled with other items in the closet.

Each part of your closet can be designed in a variety of configurations. You must determine which aspects of the given designs are most productive and effective for your own circumstances. You must decide for yourself if it is a good idea to place dresser drawers in the closet. If the drawers contain items that are worn repeatedly before they are washed—such as sweatshirts, sweatpants, jeans, and other garments that you tend to throw on after work each day or for chores and/or leisure activities—it's a waste of valuable space to stash them in a drawer unit. You would be far better served by placing them on shelves (perhaps

This alternative to the design shown on page 83 is smaller, but adds baskets and repositions the shelves and drawers.

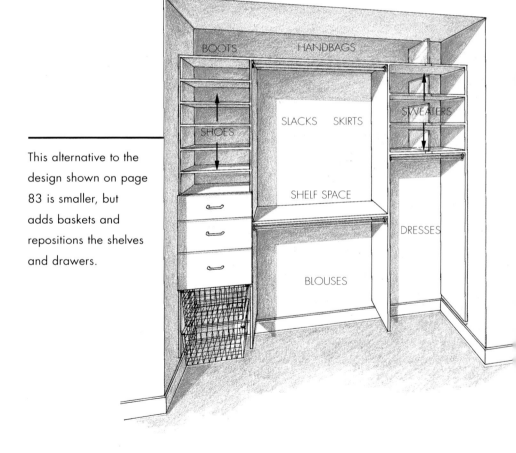

BOOTS HANDBAGS SLACKS SKIRTS SWEATERS SHOES SHELF SPACE DRESSES BLOUSES

behind a cabinet door). But the ideal way to handle these items, as well as robes and other nightwear, is to place a few small hooks in the accessible spaces along the side edges of the closet, or you could develop a system on the inside of the closet door. Also consider the manner in which the boots are stored. These boots could be folded for storage, using less shelf space. It isn't true that your boots will suffer damage from this position.

As you become more aware of your closet space and its various configurations, the problem of seasonal clothes may enter your mind. It can be distressing to look at a wardrobe that contains items you know won't be worn until the fall or spring. On the other hand, it can be a real nuisance to try to find these items in storage when the weather changes quickly. Both methods have advantages and disadvantages, and you must decide for yourself which works best for you. For more details on seasonal clothing, see the discussion in **Seasonal/Coat Closet** on pages 108–113.

Of course, the capacity of some closets simply cannot match your needs, despite all your refiguring and diagramming. But if you stick to the basic principles of organizing, your closet will at least provide as much storage space as possible.

MAN'S
CLOSET

A man's wardrobe consists, for the most part, of suits, shirts, ties, jackets, sweaters, and casual wear. You won't find the wide variety of items or lengths that are common in a woman's wardrobe. Although many feminine equivalents to a man's clothes do exist, the issue of importance is a matter of space rather than classification. A man's garments are usually longer than a woman's (except for dresses). This fact leads to a significant, though subtle, element affecting the organizing of a man's closet: Space can be used more effectively in a man's closet. All the room in a man's closet can be double-rodded, since nothing is longer than a suit coat or shirt. And the height of the shoe shelves need not extend above the height of his dress shoes or cushioned running shoes.

To organize any closet, the first step is to establish a set of standard operational procedures, or handling instructions, for the items that will go in the closet. This is a good time to make note of a special item such as a sweater that cannot be hung, yet takes up a large space when folded up. Do not deviate from these guidelines; without standard procedures, you cannot maintain control of your closet.

Remove accompanying belts from slacks. Otherwise, the garments may be stretched out of shape. Belts belong on a belt rack. When hanging slacks, match the inside seam to the outside seam at the bottom edge. Hold the

Shelves and breaking clothing into categories make for a great design in this man's closet.

slacks at the bottom, and the crease line is defined. Buttoning or zipping the slacks misaligns the crease. Simply follow the crease line to the waistband and gently mold the zipper and placket into a fold. Then fold the slacks near the middle of their length and insert them onto a hanger, keeping the fold in the center of the hanger. You may prefer to hang your

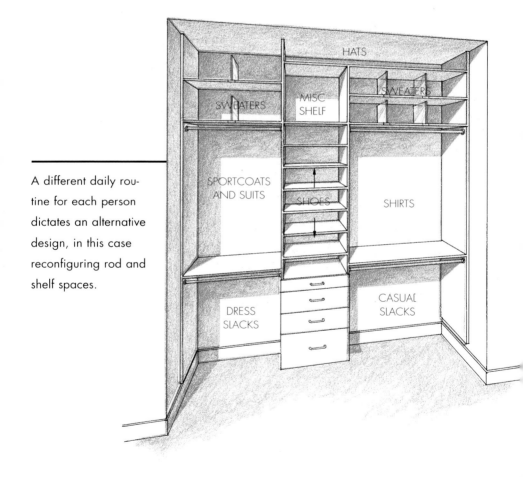

A different daily routine for each person dictates an alternative design, in this case reconfiguring rod and shelf spaces.

slacks by their full length, which calls for a type of hanger known as a clamp hanger. But be warned: These hangers might mar the cuffs of slacks by leaving pressure marks that are difficult to remove.

Save time by grouping business wear components close together in your closet.

When hanging shirts, fasten the top button, top two buttons, or every other button for the entire length of the garment. This will keep the occurrence of wrinkles and cock-eyed collars to a minimum. After putting the garment on the hanger, place the hanger on the rod so that all hangers face the same direction. Perhaps the worst habit you can get into is deliberately pulling a garment from its hanger. Instead, remove the hanger from the rod and then unbutton the garment from the hanger. Put the empty hanger in the pre-assigned workspace area.

The question of what to do with seasonal clothes usually arises sometime during the organizing process. It may seem a waste of space to have all your winter clothes hanging in your closet in the middle of July and vice versa. But storing out-of-season clothes separately can be bothersome and time-consuming, involving dry cleaning, mending, folding and packing, and then finding and unpacking the garments later. The choice of which storage method to use depends on your personal preference as well as the amount of space in your closet and the availability of extra closets elsewhere in your home.

For ideas to help make your decision see the discussion in **Seasonal/Coat Closet** on pages 108–113.

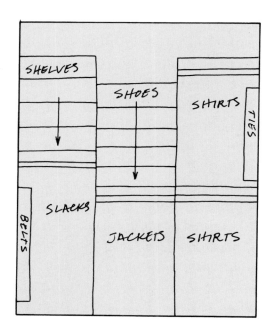

Your draft should reflect your personal needs, not what looks more dazzling.

Note in the closet shown on page 89 that all supports and appointments are kept off the floor. This adds an extra convenience: You can run the vacuum cleaner or dust mop into every corner, reaching every inch where dust collects.

Each part of your closet can be designed in a variety of configurations. You must determine which aspects of the given designs are most productive and effective for your own circumstances. Note the alternative arrangement shown in the illustration on page 90. Coming up with an alternative design requires some thought and speculation. The time spent designing an alternative is often worthwhile, since the result often may be a truly innovative finished product. The best way to get your creative juices flowing is to evaluate and compare several closet renovation projects and their special features. Eventually, you'll arrive at an arrangement that satisfies your own personal needs.

Of course, there are those occasions when no amount of refiguring or diagramming will help increase your closet's capacity enough to accommodate all your clothes and closet items. But if you adhere to the principles of organizing, your closet will at least provide the most storage space possible under the circumstances. Perhaps a small annex is all you may need to fit the last bunch of clothes. No rule says you cannot extend the principles of organizing to this extra space. So set these rules yourself and go for it!

CHILD'S
CLOSET

At preschool and nursery school, children are taught to pick up after themselves and where to put things away. You need to structure your home environment in the same way, providing simple, easy routines that a young child can follow and understand. Keep your expectations reasonable and study your child's own capabilities before initiating any system.

Toys are perhaps the most dominant items that are stored in a child's closet. A multitude of bins or boxes on the shelves can help tremendously. Try to match the size of the container to the overall dimensions of the toys it contains. Put big toys in big containers, grouping similar items together (balls in one, stuffed animals in another, bulky playthings in another). Put small toys in small containers. Be

wary of containers that allow tiny parts and pieces to slip or protrude through the container; net bags aren't a good idea. Solid duffel bags in a variety of sizes and colors work quite nicely. These bags can be hung from a peg board, or they can sit in a corner of the room.

Transparent containers with easily removable lids also work well. Then your child won't need to open every container to see the contents, and you won't hear the constant requests to find a particular toy. If you already own a generous supply of cardboard boxes, place a picture or label on the outside of the box to identify its contents. Thus, when your child

In this properly organized child's closet, toys and clothes all have their proper spot, making each item easier to find.

wants a particular plaything, he or she can go directly to the box that holds it. Involving your child in this process can go a long way in helping to instill a sense of responsibility over his or her belongings. Reinforce the corners of cardboard boxes with durable tape, or the boxes will be quickly destroyed.

Don't stack the boxes or transparent containers on top of each other; inevitably, the child will want the one on the bottom. Instead, align them horizontally so each box slides out from between the others without interference. One rule must be enforced to make this system really work well: Before your child is allowed to open a second box, the first box must be put back. It could take your child some time to become used to this routine. Once learned it will save you hours of clean-up time.

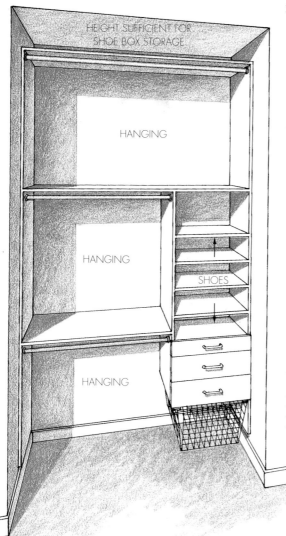

HEIGHT SUFFICIENT FOR
SHOE BOX STORAGE

HANGING

HANGING

SHOES

HANGING

Don't put the most common toy container—a toy chest with a hinged lid—in the closet. When your child is preoccupied with sorting through the goodies in the chest, he or she is likely to forget that the lid is open. The lid may come down on fingers, arms, or heads, and you'll end up calming down a crying child. The toy chest also mixes tiny toys, such as little dolls, with big toys such as basketballs. This forces your child to dump everything out on the floor, leaving you to face the mess.

Another way to keep your child's closet neat is by purchasing child-size hangers. Little plastic hangers are fatter and sturdier than wire hangers, and little hands can handle them better. The visual impact of colored hangers keeps your child's attention focused on hanging up their clothes.

This child's closet shown on page 95 uses child-size hangers for clothes and baskets for holding toys. It also raises a question that only you can decide. Who will secure and replace the hanging garments positioned on the top rod? How much control do you wish to retain? Do you want your child to acquire some independence and freedom in choosing clothes as well as the responsibility for keeping clothing neat and tidy?

If you can't afford the cost of remodeling your child's closet but still want to add extra rods for hanging clothes, an extender rod will do the trick. An extender rod hooks onto the regular clothes rod with two "arms." The arms hang down to a rod that can function as a clothes rod. Extender rods come in many shapes, sizes, and materials. Choose one that is versatile and flexible. Measure your child's arm so the extender rod hangs low enough for him or her to reach the items on the rod.

As your child ages and enters the teenage years closet reorganization will probably become necessary.

Teenagers accumulate more and more items with each birthday and Christmas. Where is everything supposed to go? If you really want to see your teen's room neat and tidy, you must provide the guiding hand. Your responsibility is to implement simple and easy routines and methods that your teenager can then follow without a lot of fuss and bother. The harder the routines and methods are, the less likely your teenager is to comply with your wishes.

As you design your teen's closet space, be sure to contemplate the actual physical maneuvers and activities of the day-to-day workings of the system. Before making any final decisions, mentally place yourself in front of the closet: Imagine the paces, motions, and rituals a particular design will require from your teenager. If the new system is harder to use than the present "system" of stashing and dropping, it isn't the solution you're looking for.

Any desire to reach a higher level of organization requires establishing realistic goals. The most you should ask of yourself or your family is a willingness to compromise to achieve your goals, but don't make the organizational system impossible to use.

If items in your teen's closet almost always end up on the floor, perhaps additional shelves and baskets for his or her many accessories are necessary. Once those items are lifted off the floor, you have created a neater look. Hanging space lost to shelves and baskets can be made up by installing two shorter rods and an extra shelf.

Use wire baskets to hold socks, underwear, T-shirts, shorts, or any other item your teen may own an excess supply of.

If your teenager is an athlete, provide a bas-

For an athletic teen, this equipment basket will make sports gear effortless to store and locate.

In this closet, more hanging space is allocated for longer clothes.

ket close to the bottom of his or her closet for storing sports equipment.

Even an excellent design can be improved. For example, perhaps the depths of some of the wire baskets could be less. This can help to deter the growth of unmanageable stacks of clothes that may be difficult to keep neat. This is part of the transition from the child's to the teen's closet.

Also, as the years go by and your teen acquires more clothes, storing his or her books, videos, and tapes may become more impractical; the shelf space inside the closet may be better used in the future for sweaters or shoes. Typically, a teenage boy's bedroom has bookcases and shelves. The books, videos, and tapes from his closet can be sensibly arranged on his bookcases and shelves. A teenager's bedroom certainly benefits from the addi-

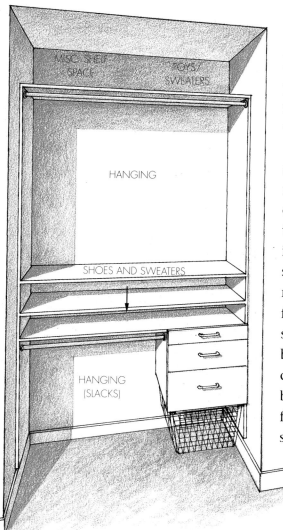

MISC. SHELF SPACE

TOYS/ SWEATERS

HANGING

SHOES AND SWEATERS

HANGING (SLACKS)

tion of more shelves, and numerous styles and sizes of shelves are readily available.

As your teenage son grows older and begins to acquire sportcoats and slacks, suits, and other "nicer" clothes, he'll soon outgrow the hanging space the present closet design provides. The down jackets and vests may eventually be moved to a family coat closet. If you and he prefer to keep his jackets and coats in the bedroom, a coat rack will hold his outer garments, freeing up closet space. The rack will also serve to hold jeans and schoolbags; better on the coat rack than on the floor or bed!

It's always a good idea to give a growing teenager compartments, pockets, and pouches for all his or her paraphernalia. An over-the-door pouch system can't be beat for promoting instant neatness when placed on the bedroom or closet door.

When a young girl reaches her teens, she may have accumulated a clutter of clothes, books, magazines, videos, accessories, stuffed animals, jewelry, and letters. The advice for space management, assigned placement, shelves, and receptacles for personal possessions is just as applicable to teen girls as it is to teen boys. The differences consist of supplying longer hanging areas of closet space for dresses and skirts; more space for sweaters, sweats, T-shirts, shoes, and purses; and a specific place for jewelry and hair accessories.

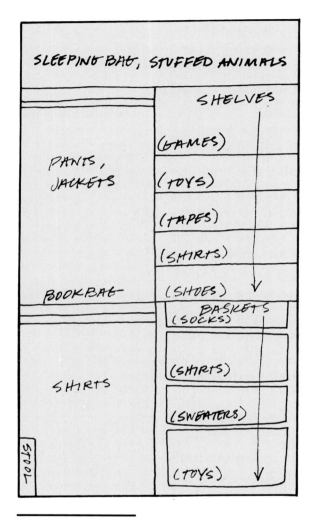

Any design for your teenager's closet must be flexible enough to meet the child's changing needs.

Your teenage daughter may not be quite willing to lock away her collection of stuffed animals acquired over the years, but you may be tired of tending to them. Something as simple as a net or rope strung from one corner to another or a pole or chain secured to the ceiling may suddenly lift those furry adorables out from underfoot.

As a teenage girl develops her individual taste—especially in jewelry—the accessories she has today may or may not please her sense of style tomorrow. To handle a great quantity of accessories and jewelry, a drawer organizer and accessory board provide storage space and promote neatness. Inside the dresser drawer itself, try installing many small boxes. Each small box should contain only one piece of jewelry or a group of similar pieces. A good organizing method for these items is to keep each category of items separate and each color within each category separate. Put these small boxes on a piece of cardboard or inside a larger, shallow box (such as the top of a shoe box). This creates a layer that is easily removed so that the layer underneath is then accessible.

One of the greatest ways to provide shelving in a teenage girl's room—especially as a display for books or a doll collection—is to install a row of Lucite shelves along the upper perimeter of her bedroom. The shelves themselves are transparent and coordinate with any decor. The books or dolls are then placed in a location that is otherwise unused.

Any closet system for a teenager, boy or girl, should have the ability to change, because teenagers usually change from one year to the next in their interests, style, associations, and preferences. Keep this in mind and provide flexibility with as many portable, nonfixed, nonstructured items as you can. All things are possible with a bit of forethought and a view to long-range developments and short-term fads.

LINEN
CLOSET

▬

Everyone knows a "linen closet" isn't strictly a closet for linens. An assortment of articles constantly vie for a slice of space. These items cause confusion, edge other items off the shelves, or conceal the objects that sit behind them. If your linen closet held only linens, it might be spacious enough. But then what would you do with the medicines, toiletries, cleaning supplies, and tissues that are normally kept in a linen closet?

A door rack such as the one shown on page 106 is perfect for holding many items, consigning them to a more manageable area of space. This should empty at least one or two shelves of the linen closet, which can now be used for linens. Be sure to arrange the objects on the door rack methodically, or the rack won't be working to its full potential. To obtain the maximum use from the rack, designate a specific role to each shelf.

This rack does have one structural drawback. The evenly spaced openings of the shelves allow smaller bottles and jars to fall through the gaps or sit cockeyed between the struts. As a remedy, place shallow, narrow boxes on the shelves. Each box holds the contents of the shelf. In addition, a box—complete with contents—can be removed from the shelf and carried to anyplace it is needed. This rack system adds another advantage. Since each shelf holds all the items of one category, you know the quantity you own. This will help prevent stockpiling: owning three or four containers of the same product.

Whether or not the door rack is a viable

Linen closets are usually small and narrow, but lots of shelves make room for linens and bath items.

option for your linen closet, you still must decide what to do with the existing shelves inside the closet. The shelves are unlikely to be positioned at favorable heights, and there is probably too much space between shelves, which promotes unwieldy stacks of items. The items on the bottom or at the back of the stacks are the most difficult to obtain.

The large expanses of space should be divided into smaller, more workable sections that are compatible with the size and shape of your folded towels and bedding. Portable shelves are perfect for this. If you decide to remodel your linen closet, give serious thought to shelves that can be adjusted for height so you remain flexible in case your needs change. And don't let a remodeling expert convince you that a shelf with a 16-inch depth is preferable to a shelf with a 12-inch depth. In a linen closet, that extra four inches will always capture mismatched objects. These objects will end up in seclusion at the back of the shelf, creating a place that contains nothing but clutter. Also,

TISSUES

FEMININE
HYGIENE

MEDICATIONS

BATH PRODUCTS

ORAL HYGIENE

SKIN AND
HAIR CARE

CLEANING
SUPPLIES

A door rack employs otherwise unused space. The rack can hold many bath items.

with shallower shelves, more room will be available for a door rack or other storage ideas.

What if you don't have a linen closet or you'd like to preserve its space for towels, wash clothes, and bedding only? There are several ways to approach this problem. A self-supporting shelf system can be set up anywhere you deem appropriate. Or bed linens could be placed in the guest bedroom, on a shelf in that room's closet or in under-the-bed storage drawers.

As stated earlier, linen closets are generally a multipurpose storage area. Many odds and ends—such as vacuum cleaners or ironing boards—can conceivably find their way into a linen closet. It can seem like a lot to ask from one small closet. There isn't any established theory for choosing which closet, room, or nook will hold your vacuum cleaner or ironing board. So, you have the option to work with whatever space suits you the best.

If the linen closet is your choice to hold a vacuum cleaner or ironing board, you'll need compact racks that can handle a very specific need. The linen closet often leaves little usable workspace. For example, an ironing board rack may be well suited, both in size and shape, to the confined areas of a linen closet. Other items that could be stored in this area include: miniature tools, mops, brooms, buckets, and plungers.

SEASONAL/ COAT

CLOSET

As you organize the closets in your home, especially the closets that hold your personal wardrobe, the problem of seasonal clothes and outer garments will loom larger. If the space in your closet is at a premium, using that space to store clothes that won't be worn until the spring or the fall can seem like a waste. On the other hand, digging those seasonal clothes and outer garments out of storage can be a real nuisance. Most likely they'll be located in some inconvenient spot. And once you get them unpacked, you'll discover that many need dry cleaning or ironing or mending. Little will actually make its way into

your closet for quite some time. And then there are the clothes that are now out of season. You'll have to fold and pack them up and store them somewhere for six months. The choice is completely up to you, but it is probably easier to keep the majority of your wardrobe together in one location than dealing with the complexity of separate storage.

Most seasonal/coat closets end up storing more items other than just coats such as skis, camera bags, blankets, hats, scarves, and mittens.

A closet can contain your extra seasonal clothing if you follow the principles of organization. Sad to say, there are some closets that simply cannot do the job no matter how much refiguring and diagramming you do.

You're fortunate if you have a spare closet elsewhere in your home. This is a blessing for two reasons. You only need to search one of two closets to find every article you own. Also, clothing remains on hangers, which eliminates the inevitable wrinkles your garments suffer every time they're folded and stored for any length of time.

Coat rods that slip in and out of the bracket make for easy adjustments and additions.

It can't be stressed enough—whenever possible keep clothes on hangers! This is a basic rule of organizing.

One possible spare closet that can serve you well for seasonal clothes as well as for outer garments is the coat closet. This is one of the easiest closets in the home to revamp. Just take a good hard look at the lengths of the coats. Coats should not be treated as though they were all identical. You wouldn't want to hang a long trench coat next to a leather pilot's jacket. The difference in length wastes about a third of the hanging space. But the situation is easily corrected. By placing a second permanent rod at a lower level as shown in the photograph on page 109, the closet gains much more space for hanging coats. Or you could use it to hang your seasonal clothes, such as flannel shirts or short sleeve cotton blouses.

After alleviating the cramped quarters for your outer garments, the next step is to focus on outerwear accessories. Gather up the scattered and lost mates for your gloves and mittens and then keep them in one place. Separate baskets for scarves, knit hats, and mittens and gloves may work well. Another alternative is a "mitten pouch." It can be nothing more ingenious than a new application of a clear vinyl shoe bag. Hang it from the side wall or the inside of the door. The clear vinyl pouches provide easy access and visibility.

Umbrellas needn't rest on the shelf. Hanging them from a clothes rod is very convenient. If the rod can't spare the space, a few clamps incorporated on the side walls of the closet or on the inside of the door will also hold umbrellas.

Of course, a seasonal/coat closet usually ends up holding more than just coats and out-of-season clothing. You'll find hats, boots, table-leaves, golf clubs, skis, and other outlandish gear that gradually gravitates to this closet. This closet may not be the best place

Wherever you keep your out-of-season clothing, vinyl garment bags offer protection from dust and dirt.

for these items, but this may be the only closet you have for them!

Quite often, if there is a coat closet, it is inadequate because it's either too small or too far away from the front door. This inconvenience unfortunately may cause you to toss your coat and hat on nearby chairs or tables. These items wouldn't create so much disorder if they were hung closer to the door you use. A coat rack would furnish a convenient and attractive way to hang your everyday outerwear; the coats you only wear occasionally can be kept in the coat closet.

Not everyone has the luxury of a coat closet or other spare closet. This is often the case in older homes that are remodeled into apartments or condominiums. The next best option is to install a closet rod, permanent or portable, where you can. Scads of hanging racks are available, in every conceivable size and shape. These racks can fit in any nook or cranny of your home, turning an unused space into a "spare closet" for seasonal storage. You can protect your garments from dust by enclosing them in a vinyl bag with a zippered front as shown on the opposite page. Another measure of protection can be added by adapting the closet rod to include mothproofing.

There is one remaining alternative for storing seasonal belongings. If your only choice is a box, invest in an assortment of quilted vinyl cases with zippers. Protect the clothing that will be stored in a box. Fold and pack the clothes carefully, encasing them in protective fabric or tissue paper. If your inventory of seasonal belongings is large, place only a specific category (such as sweaters) in each box. If you wind up with several boxes, a good idea would be to label them for easy accessibility. The boxes won't need adhesive labels to identify the contents if you use color-coded boxes.

A variation on the box idea that has some distinct advantages is the under-the-bed storage system. Simply roll the drawer out from underneath your bed and remove the cover. This method keeps your clothing inside, where it won't be exposed to extreme heat and cold or various creatures. And you'll never have to carry another heavy box from the bedroom to the shed or attic and vice versa.

LAUNDRY
FACILITIES

Wouldn't it tickle your fancy to create a wall unit for your laundry area like the one shown on the next page? Unfortunately, this is usually just wishful thinking. However, you could pick the most desirable traits seen here and adapt them to fit your own circumstances.

Think about the greatest difficulty you encounter on laundry day. Is it finding a place to fold or hang clothes? Is it needing bins for dirty laundry rather than having heaps on the floor? Or is it having enough shelf space for all the detergents, bleaches, water softeners, and pre-soak products you use? Determine your priorities first, especially if the space around the washer and dryer is limited. Sometimes a written list works well by putting things into perspective.

An overhead shelving or cabinet unit is one smart move to make, since it demands no floor space. The unit can either run the length of the area, covering both the washer and dryer as they sit side by side, or you can include a rod for hanging clothes fresh from the dryer or clothes from the washer that must drip-dry. A system for presorting dirty clothes, such as wire baskets, can be a big help during the week and on laundry day. An extra touch is the addition of countertop work space above the baskets, which supplies an excellent place for folding clothes, removing spots and stains, and compiling clean clothes for distribution throughout your home. As always, base these decisions, after careful consideration, on your personal priorities and needs.

An ideal laundry area has room for everything. Most likely, you'll have to make some compromises.

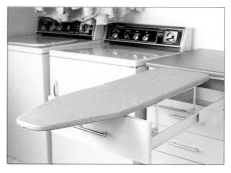

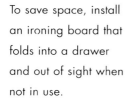

To save space, install an ironing board that folds into a drawer and out of sight when not in use.

Many of today's fashions dictate fabrics that demand a lot of attention and care. In the past it wasn't as important to properly drip-dry dresses and shirts or to shape, mold, and lay out sweaters, slacks, skirts, and blouses on a flat surface for drying. These garments may need to remain in this position for at least two days before they're fully dry. How do you obtain this much space for this much time? Based on the available space in and around your washer and dryer, choose a suitable drying rack for your space's configuration. Racks that fold up for compact storage when not in use are of particular value especially in tight areas with very limited space.

An iron and ironing board are more necessary today than ever before, again due to the fabrics dictated by fashion. If you have enough space to keep your ironing board open and ready for pressing, you're one of the lucky ones.

Most individuals are faced with the dilemma of whether they should put the ironing board in the crack between the wall and the refrigerator, shove it against the basement steps, or find some other equally inconvenient spot. Manufacturers have contrived a variety of compact, collapsible, self-contained storage systems for concealing or containing the ironing board. They range from a unit that springs from a box to a unit that springs from a drawer (see the two photographs on the opposite page) to a unit that transforms itself into a chair when it isn't being used.

Sometimes the laundry facilities have a room to themselves, not just a recessed closet-size area in a hallway, kitchen, or corner of the basement. If this is the case, there may be room for plenty of cabinets for storage. Cabinet storage can be improved by installing racks and plenty of shelves. Then the laundry room becomes the area for stowing all your cleaning supplies, such as scouring cleansers, window cleaners, and furniture polish, thus freeing up space in another area of your home. Using the techniques and ideas recommended, you may end up with more room than you imagined.

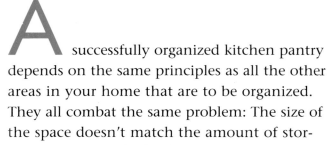

KITCHEN
PANTRY

A successfully organized kitchen pantry depends on the same principles as all the other areas in your home that are to be organized. They all combat the same problem: The size of the space doesn't match the amount of storage needed. The food items kept in your kitchen pantry need to be regulated through the organizing system you use and through the size of the space they inhabit. For instance, when canned goods are stored willy-nilly on one shelf or another, it's no wonder you can't keep tabs on them. The pantry must be organized to ultimately create many smaller sections of space. This will keep all the items in your pantry—canned goods, spices, chips, dishes, pasta, flour, and other miscella-

Baskets that roll out on wheels can hold bulky items and provide easy access to these items.

Store items in your pantry by category. A well-designed pantry can hold much more than food, including dishes and cookware.

neous kitchen goods—more visible, accessible, and controlled.

Items should be kept separate: soups from boxed cereals, spices from pastas, pots and pans from dishes, and so on. Each distinct and different category should be treated as a separate entity. You might try placing the items on the shelves in alphabetical order: appetizers at one end and finishing with vegetables at the opposite end. Routinely returning items and storing replacements in the same organized area they were found saves time and money in the not-so-long run.

As you contemplate various methods for re-organizing the space in the pantry, you'll probably review the "slide-out" basket drawer.

These types of baskets are definite space savers and can hold plenty of items. The bottom of the baskets may need a piece of Lucite, cardboard, or plywood to provide a level surface. The slide-out drawer is useful for bagged or bulky items such as pasta or chips. Smaller, shallower baskets may provide better access for smaller containers of condiments or spices.

You might consider adding some stackable bins to the pantry, but they are advisable only for storing such bulk items as potatoes or dried beans. It's fine to reach into the bin and grab a handful of potatoes, but this would hardly be acceptable if you wanted crackers and pulled out a box of cake mix instead! These bins are a good way to use the pantry's floor space. Stackable shelving units may also work well in unused floor space. If you have enough space of the correct shape, the floor area of the pantry may also be the perfect spot for a recycling center or a miniature wine cellar.

An innovative variation shown in the photograph on page 119 is the use of the corner for shelves. As in any closet space, the corner is not very useful. But in this case the shelving turns the corner into a productive, spacious place for many items. Divide existing shelf space in the pantry. This will double the amount of usable shelf space and make that shelf space a more manageable and functional storage area.

Pantries, like laundry rooms, often serve duty in the never ending search for storage space. There are various ways and means to perform this extra duty properly and efficiently. Some racks fit snugly and compactly to the side walls of a pantry, to the inside of a cabinet door, or underneath a shelf. Examine the wide variety of racks that are available and decide if any meet your needs. The pantry is also often the final resting place for extra sets of silverware, china, or stemware. The space inside the pantry can hold these items if you use various types of racks available at many stores. It's also possible the pantry could supply the only storage area for cleaning supplies. If that is the case, an all-in-one portable cleaning cart is a prime example of effective, efficient use of space.

And what if you have no pantry at all? You can create your own by either purchasing a floor model unit or improvising one from an existing cabinet.

HOME
OFFICE

I t's a rare exception when a spare closet exists that can be converted into a home office. Most likely, you'll need to devise a system in a corner or a portion of a room. So you'll have to harmonize the office with the surroundings by providing attractive storage. It is imperative that a clean and uncluttered environment emerge from the present situation. The storage solutions you use should be influential in maintaining order and efficiency.

Start with the largest components: desk, shelves, work surfaces, and filing cabinets. Choose the components and pieces that meet your specific needs. These decisions, of course, depend on the amount of space you have to work with. If the available space is too small

to consider a lot of improvements and components, you'll have to use scaled-down versions of the components to attain a functioning area for work and storage. For instance, a file cabinet with an overlapping desktop would furnish a modest work and storage facility for the bare essentials for keeping track of mundane household accounts. Something that simple could possibly handle a small part-time endeavor but would hardly serve as a serious full-time in-home business operation. Again, a lone drafting table would suffice for an occasional project, but for full-time employment, an abundant system of shelves and drawers would also be needed.

The home office is an area where compromise in space is probably necessary.

Once you've ascertained how to acquire sufficient room for typewriters, telephones, computers, modems, lamps, and the like, you must determine the best way to store the many smaller, supportive materials and supplies. These materials and supplies—which range from pens to reference books to tax statements—have different characteristics, shapes, sizes, and uses. You must also determine how often you need these items: at a moment's notice, infrequently, once a month, or only annually as a source of reference. This will dramatically affect what methods of storage are best to use.

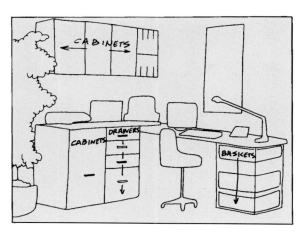

As with any organizing process, start with a simple hand-drawn diagram of the intended design for your home office.

For daily rituals, you'll want efficiency in drawer space and with the incoming and outgoing systems. Always divide drawers into distinct compartments that prevent the contents from interfering with each other. Stationery supply shops have a number of drawer dividers, but you may be able to design and divide the drawers yourself using boxes, inserts, or other creative solutions. Any home office system should have categories for current, incoming, outgoing, pending, to-do-today, as well as a tickler for follow-up. This system helps you keep track of where and when, and you'll spend less time trying to remember and more time in productive activities. Generally, the more categories you create to mark these distinctions, the better the system will be.

Reminder books and books that keep account of data are also beneficial. To name just a few: a household inventory book with sleeves for photographs of your possessions and space for a description, cost, and purchase date; a book of keys with slots for keys to your car, boat, cabinet, cosmetic case, or Grandma's front door; a special occasion reminder book so you'll never miss another birthday; photo albums and scrapbooks for all those photographs and negatives.

Simply stacking a pile of mismatched, unrelated papers into a huge box and filing it on the top shelf isn't organizing. Just when you think you won't need those items anymore, you probably will. As long as you're going to the trouble of putting papers, policies, and receipts in a box, divide the papers by category and put each category in a separate box. Be sure to label each box for contents. For space conservation, incorporate the smaller uniform boxes into one larger box and put that box on the top shelf.

GARAGE/
WORKSHOP

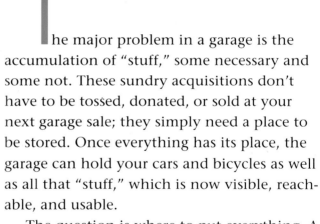

The major problem in a garage is the accumulation of "stuff," some necessary and some not. These sundry acquisitions don't have to be tossed, donated, or sold at your next garage sale; they simply need a place to be stored. Once everything has its place, the garage can hold your cars and bicycles as well as all that "stuff," which is now visible, reachable, and usable.

The question is where to put everything. A garage provides more wall space than floor space, so it's an easy task to systematically assign and arrange that space. The ceiling is also a valuable resource for storage space. With the insertion of a few well-placed hooks, the ceiling can hold bicycles, ladders, and luggage out of the way. A storage shelf installed from

Recycling bins hold aluminum, glass, and newsprint and keep clutter to a minimum.

the ceiling is great for items that are used infrequently or seasonally, such as camping gear, outdoor Christmas decorations or lights, or window screens and storm doors.

Built-in shelves provide plenty of space for paint cans, spray bottles, mulch, buckets, automotive supplies, flower pots, and boxes and bags of all descriptions. Make sure you arrange them on the shelves by category, putting like items together. It's helpful to confine smaller items in a system of drawers attached to the shelves or in boxes and bins that sit on the shelves. Both drawers and bins or boxes should have attached identification labels.

Your garage often holds more than your car. Storage units on the walls can become a hobby center.

As you sort through everything in your garage, you'll quickly realize that many items need more specific and detailed handling. Or you may decide to designate a specific area as a workshop or as storage for your particular hobby or sport. Your sport may be tennis, ski-

ing, golf, bicycling, or some other activity. A neat and tidy look, combined with a great deal of storage, can be achieved with this equipment displayed on the walls rather than scattered on the floor.

If you're simply looking for a place and a way to organize the tools, nails, and wrenches you use periodically, a rack or portable tool box may do the trick. This can be kept in the garage or in the basement, depending on your needs and space.

Tools and household accessories can be kept tidy and orga- nized in your garage.

With today's concern over the environ- ment, recycling is becoming more common. Recycling bins are most often kept on the floor, taking up valuable space. You can at least control and reduce the amount of space occupied by using stackable bins. Adding a hand cart keeps you from having to make two or three trips to the curb on trash day. Just wheel the entire three-piece unit—with its separate loads of glass, aluminum, and plas- tic—out of the garage and to the street.